LIVING *with* IBD & IBS

LIVING *with* IBD & IBS

✦

A Personal Journey of Success

Elizabeth A. Roberts

iUniverse, Inc.
New York Lincoln Shanghai

LIVING *with* IBD & IBS
A Personal Journey of Success

iUniverse books may be ordered through booksellers or by contacting:

iUniverse
2021 Pine Lake Road, Suite 100
Lincoln, NE 68512
www.iuniverse.com
1-800-Authors (1-800-288-4677)

ISBN-13: 978-0-595-40293-9 (pbk)
ISBN-13: 978-0-595-84669-6 (ebk)
ISBN-10: 0-595-40293-3 (pbk)
ISBN-10: 0-595-84669-6 (ebk)

Printed in the United States of America

To John…
for your ever-present
patience, love, and good humor

Contents

Foreword

This book is the author's recollection of her personal experiences of learning to live *with* IBD (Inflammatory Bowel Disease) and IBS (Irritable Bowel Syndrome). The author is not a physician, nurse, dietitian, homeopath, psychologist, or psychiatrist. The experiences described herein are hers and hers alone and are not to be substituted for treatment or care by licensed, professional health care providers. The author does not advocate the use of any treatments, medications, herbs, or supplements for the treatment of these, or any other, illnesses or diseases.

The events, conversations, and recollections in this book are based solely on the author's own memory and knowledge of said events.

Introduction

Sitting on the front deck of our Lake Tahoe home one crisp fall evening in 2001, my husband and I took in the beautiful view of the blazing orange sun as it set over the Sierra Nevada mountain range.

John reminisced about our past four years living at Lake Tahoe. "It's been a big change from Washington, D.C.," he said.

While I listened to his words, my mind whirled through the huge number of changes that had, indeed, entered my life in the past few years. The enormity of it hit me all at once.

I'm only 33, I thought, *I have an incurable colon disease which doctors only somewhat understand and, I have no choice but to simply live with it and the awful effects it can bring into my day-to-day life.*

The warmth of John's hand on mine shook me from my thoughts. "What are you thinking about so hard?" he asked.

God, did I want to verbalize what I was thinking? To possibly open the door to the demon that had been ever-present in not only my life, but both of our lives, for the past three years?

I took a few deep breaths, choked back the tears that were welling in my eyes and in a barely audible whisper shared my thoughts with my husband.

"I was thinking about my colitis," I told him. "I know I've been living with and dealing with this disease for the past three years, but it only just hit me tonight that it will never really go away and I'll never be the same person I was before my diagnosis."

Our silence was broken only when the tears I'd been holding back finally gushed forth. Big, wet elephant tears rolled down my cheeks and splashed onto my lap. My husband let me cry for a few minutes then tenderly gazed into my blood-shot eyes.

"You're right, things aren't the same as before your diagnosis," he said a little too matter-of-factly. "And you aren't the same person you were before 1998. The past three years have brought huge changes for you, for me, for both of us. And while some days have been harder than others, they haven't all been bad, Lizzy. You know that."

As I stared at the wood decking beneath my feet, the many, many changes of the past years played through my mind like a slide show.

Bouts of urgent and unrelenting diarrhea...cramps...fatigue...confusion...fear...the elimination diet...the B.R.A.T. diet...acidophilus...fenu greek...slippery elm...aloe vera juice...learning to relax...learning to meditate...learning about Reiki and how to practice it on myself...doctors...nurses...energy healers...Internet chat rooms...websites...resource books...natural food stores...alternative medicine magazines...hours of research about IBD, microscopic colitis & IBS...realizing the importance of knowing my body and listening to what it needs...asking for help...asking for space...giving myself time to learn about the new me...learning to accept my new life and who I now am...realizing my disease doesn't have total control over me unless I allow it to...

With his index finger under my chin, John gently lifted my head until I was looking him in the eye again.

"Think how much more we both understand about what's going on with you. Think about how much more in control of the colitis and IBS you are today than even a year ago. You've learned so much about yourself, your body, and what makes you sick as well as how to make yourself better. Look at what we've learned about us, as a couple, and what's truly important in life."

He paused, gracing my forehead with a light butterfly kiss.

"It hasn't always been fun," he continued. "I'll be the first to admit that some periods in the past few years have been downright frightening and frustrating. But I really do believe you've come out the other end of this disease a lot better, in some ways, than you went in."

"Come out the other end?" I asked as I wiped away my tears and mustered a smile.

As I considered his words, more thoughts of the past years swirled through my mind. As I slowly pulled myself out of my self-induced pity-party, I realized he was right. These past years had been filled with a ton of hard times and scary episodes. But there were also plenty of times that had been full of learning, understanding, experimentation and even rejuvenation. Yes, I admitted, my disease was still with me and probably always would be, unless some miraculous gene therapy is discovered some day that cures it. I even remembered to remind myself that the colitis and IBS were no longer demons lurking in my closet ready to pounce and debilitate me as they once had been. Instead, I now had a good understanding of how my disease worked, as well as my body's reaction to it. I had my "tool box" of coping mechanisms that I can call upon when a "bad stomach day" hits. And, as unbelievable as it seemed, John was right. In some ways, I truly was healthier today, both physically and spiritually, than I ever imagined was possible three years before.

◆   ◆   ◆

I decided to write this book for the many other people who have been or will be diagnosed with Inflammatory Bowel Disease (IBD) and Irritable Bowel Syndrome (IBS) so that they can know there is life—perhaps even a better life—after receiving one or both of these diagnoses.

When I was first able to put a name to my illness I was scared, I was frustrated and I was angry. I read everything I could lay my hands on about both IBD and IBS—which, at the time, wasn't anywhere near as much information as is available today. While I found a number of books and information on internet websites that gave me a lot of medical and technical information about IBD, I found very little practical or useful day-to-day coping information. I wished I could find other people who might understand me from the human side, rather than the medical side of my disease. I longed to find someone with whom I could commiserate, someone who could know how I felt not only physically but emotionally as well. And while my husband, friends and family lent their sympathy and understanding, they just couldn't understand the illness I was learning to live with.

So, this book is written for the millions of people worldwide who live with all forms of IBD and IBS every day. My hope is that you will find hope in my successes, reality in my distresses, and tips and information that will spur you on to living as full and contented a life as possible despite your illness.

This book is about…

> …Getting past the denial, anger and humiliation that can accompany a diagnosis of IBD or IBS.

> …Facing the fears about the physical symptoms of IBD and IBS.

> …Providing ideas that may help you adjust your lifestyle to living with IBD and IBS.

> …Helping your family and friends adjust to the new you.

> …Using alternative "tools" to forge your new life—from altering your diet to homeopathy to practicing Reiki and meditation.

> …Living positively and fully with a chronic illness like IBD or IBS.

◆   ◆   ◆

At the end of each chapter there is a TIPS AND INFORMATION section where I have provided resources that can help you take control of your IBD or IBS, rather than allowing it to take control of you. Whether you have been coping with one or both of these diseases for years, but still can't live positively and fully, or are newly diagnosed, this book has something that will help start you on your path to healing and reclaiming your life.

As you read about my journey, you will realize that learning to live with illness entails working through the five stages of grief—denial, anger, bargaining, depression and acceptance. I have come to believe that this an important process to go through as you allow your old self to be replaced with your new self. Do not deny yourself the opportunity to feel and work through each stage of your emotions while you learn to live *with* your disease.

I embarked on this process and am now able to acknowledge that I may never fully understand this illness, or have 100% control over the symptoms. Even though the symptoms will most likely affect me for the rest of my life to one degree or another, I have learned some crucial skills and coping mechanisms that allow me to live *with* my disease. I have also learned to realize what truly is and is not important to happiness in my life. Just as importantly, I have found from sharing my experiences with others who have these and other chronic illnesses that my knowledge can help others who are either at a crossroads in a current illness, or just beginning their journey to self-discovery. I have realized that the most important part of coping with illness, any illness, is realizing you are *not* alone.

I do not claim to have all the answers about IBD, IBS or any other illnesses. I wish I did. Also, I am not an M.D., an R.N., or a registered dietitian. I am a woman with a Bachelor of Arts degree in Journalism from the University of Wisconsin, Milwaukee, who is adept at researching information and lives *with* IBD and IBS every day. And because of my illnesses, I continue to learn something more about myself each day. There are days I sail right through without a glitch, hardly realizing that my life has had to change. Then there are days with huge gales and gusting winds that threaten to knock me down for the count. If it were not for my journey of self-education and introspection throughout the past five years I believe that I could have been blown overboard a long time ago, gasping for air and floundering to stay afloat in a huge sea of fear, exhaustion, misdirected emotion and feelings of helplessness and hopelessness.

I am so much further ahead today, both physically and emotionally, than when I was first diagnosed in 1998. Whether the demon lurking in your closet is IBD, IBS, or any of the other chronic autoimmune diseases—arthritis, fibromyalgia, chronic fatigue syndrome, or celiac disease—that can creep up and take over yourself and possibly your life, my hope is that my experiences will guide and inspire you to begin your own journey of self-preservation.

As your journey begins with this book, realize that what has been helpful to me or others you know may or may not prove helpful to you. There are no set rules that we can all follow to successful healing. The same disease can and will afflict each individual, as just that, an individual. However, as you come along with me on my journey, know that you can take control of your illness and your life. For today, tomorrow and hopefully the next day, realize that you are not alone, and that you are the best tool you possess to help and heal yourself. Try my suggestions, seek out one or two of the hundreds, thousands, or possibly millions of people who can truly understand whatever illness it is you are learning to live with, and embark on your journey today.

My journey continues every day and my wish is that you will find the hope and wisdom in it that I have.

1

B.C.: Before Colitis

My life B.C.—before colitis, that is—now seems unreal.

After I completed my college degree at the University of Wisconsin, Milwaukee in June of 1990, I immediately landed a dream job as a writer and researcher for a Washington, D.C. political newsletter, *The Cook Political Report*. The newsletter and my new boss were highly respected and renowned throughout Washington, D.C.'s political and lobbying scenes. The monthly newsletter reported on each and every congressional, senatorial and gubernatorial election taking place at any given time. We wrote the newsletter's narrative from interviews and information my boss and I gathered through daily contact with political candidates, campaign managers, pollsters and political party heads.

My life as a 20-something politico was launched. Days started at the office at 8:00 a.m. and were filled with long hours and hard but exciting work. I met Senators, Congressmen, Governors, political strategists, advertisers, Capitol Hill staffers and fellow journalists. My boss, Charlie Cook, and I spent one meeting with the somewhat wacky but brilliant James Carville before he became a household name working on Bill Clinton's 1992 Presidential campaign and on CNN's *Hardball*. His antics during our 1991 meeting were so off the wall I remember wondering whether he was truly brilliant or perhaps a bit unstable. My first job's duties also took me to the beautiful marble buildings of Congress, the U.S. Capitol, the Library of Congress and the Supreme Court, all of which I had only previously seen in books or on television. They were so much more beautiful and grandiose in person. Many business lunches took place at hot D.C. hangouts such as Red, Hot, & Blue, one of Capitol Hill's most popular lunching spots, renowned for its tangy and delicious Carolina-style BBQ, or hob-knobbing at Mr. K's Chinese restaurant in D.C.'s swanky K Street corridor.

My next job took me to a Kennedy family non-profit organization called Very Special Arts. The organization was similar in scope to Special Olympics, but instead of sports it focused on giving people with disabilities the opportunity to work with the arts. Through my public relations position with the organization doors were opened to me in the various worlds of art, music and celebrities.

I literally pinched myself the evening I stood outside the hotel suite door of jazz great Wynton Marsalis. I was there to escort Mr. Marsalis to The Kennedy Center where he would host our Young Soloists program and present the winning musicians with their awards. I punched the suite's doorbell. Before I fully realized what was happening, a boxer clad Wynton Marsalis answered the door himself.

"I was hoping you were the valet with my pants," he replied after I introduced myself.

He invited me in. Still clad only in his boxers, a dress shirt and socks, he proceeded to play the piano, while I sat on one of the numerous luxurious couches populating the hotel suite living room listening and sipping a Coke he had served me himself. If I had expected a pretentious celebrity, the evening I spent with him proved me wrong. Wynton Marsalis was an engaging, down-to-earth gentleman who enjoyed using his celebrity to educate children, men, and women alike about the one thing he holds dear—jazz.

Meeting Wyland, a spectacular marine mammal artist, was another dream come true for me in these years B.C. Throughout my childhood and now into my adulthood, my first love had always been marine mammals. I was fortunate enough to play a major role in organizing Wyland's public relations activities at Washington, D.C.'s National Zoo during his "17 Cities in 17 Weeks" East Coast tour. As he had been doing for years, he painted a life-size mural of whales and bottleneck dolphins on a wall near the entrance to the National Zoo. While the Zoo wall was smaller than most of his previous murals, he realized the importance of the mural because of the huge number of people who visit the National Zoo each year.

I also traveled with Wyland to New York City where he mesmerized hundreds of onlookers at New York City's Port Authority bus station. He is an amazing artist to watch because he uses an airbrush to create life-sized underwater scenes of marine mammals and undersea life. The 30x60-foot piece of artwork at the Port Authority took Wyland a mere afternoon to begin and complete.

But those were just my days. When work ended, friends, activities, and sports filled my nights as well as my weekends. Afternoons found me bicycling the miles of trails that wind their way along the Potomac River or hiking the trails at Great Falls and Shenandoah National Park. Meandering through the many splendid museums of Washington, D.C.'s mall also ranked high on my list of things to do as well taking in the magical beauty of the Jefferson, Lincoln and Washington monuments in the summer's humid evening starlight. When darkness fell I met friends at nightclubs like Blue's Alley, the 219 Club and the Birchmere. Or, we might while away the evening hours chatting and sampling different beers at places like the Capitol City Brewery at Union Station or the Union Street Brewery in Alexandria, Virginia. The options for dinners out and nightlife are endless in the D.C. area and I definitely did my best to try them all.

I was living the high-powered kind of life I had heard about, and it seemed perfect. There was no time, or reason, to slow down. I never once considered, or appreciated, the freedom I had to come, to go, to simply do as I pleased. I simply took my life as it was for granted, as we all seem to do when things are going well. Even when I was ill with viral spinal meningitis, not once, but twice during these years, I could barely stand to be in the hospital "doing nothing."

During these seven busy and exciting B.C. years I was fortunate to meet and fall in love with my future husband. John and I met while working for *The McLaughlin Group*, a popular political television show I had watched with my family as a young girl. Our early flirtations were spent munching Snickers candy bars and drinking Coca-Colas from the vending machines in the control room of NBC's Washington, D.C. television studio. The rest of our courtship included numerous evenings each week playing tennis in the Alexandria, Virginia twilight and muggy haze that enveloped the city in the summer. We would meet each other at various after-work gatherings. Performances at The Kennedy Center, receptions on Capitol Hill, dinners at popular D.C. hang-outs like The Occidental Restaurant or Old Ebbitt Grill and cocktail receptions with D.C.'s political elite at foreign embassies filled our nights together.

While politics and public relations are both challenging and rewarding occupations, they can also become your entire life. By the time we married in 1996, John and I were both feeling antsy with our careers, as well as with the hubbub of the city, and we wanted to have more time for ourselves. While D.C. had been good to both of us, we decided to take our lives in a completely different direction. Throughout our years of dating, a common theme repeatedly revealed itself to us. We both dreamed of making our livings writing, traveling extensively abroad, and someday settling down in Spain or Italy.

Contrary to logic, we decided to take a huge leap that we hoped would start us on our journey. We quit our jobs, cancelled the lease on the house we were renting and bad farewell to our friends and John's son who was living with his mother in a nearby neighborhood. We knew we were taking huge risks professionally, monetarily and personally but we were determined to at least try our new lifestyle. When we told friends and family our plan we were mainly greeted with reactions of disbelief and humor.

"You mean you're actually going to voluntarily give up your jobs here to go live in the mountains and write?" one friend asked. "Write what? Once you leave this town you won't have anything to write about. Plus, you'll be blacklisted as drop-outs. You'll never be able to return."

We understood where our friend was coming from. He wasn't telling us anything we hadn't already considered ourselves a hundred times. Some days John and I thought our idea to move to the West coast to a "cabin" in the woods was the best idea we'd ever had and wondered why we hadn't done it sooner. The next day we'd walk around our Virginia home sniping at each other because of the fear of the adventure we were about to embark on.

But, in April of 1997 we did leave our jobs, signed the papers on our new Lake Tahoe home, shoved ourselves, our two dogs, our luggage and laptop into our Mazda and spent the next five days driving through 13 states and 2,700 miles of beautiful highway and country roads that I'd never seen before. This was our Jack Kerouac road trip, adventuring to our unknown futures. Little did I know that my personal adventure would be filled with some of the biggest challenges of my life.

2

Changes—Good and Bad

Our first year in Tahoe was a world of newness and wonderful experiences for me. I felt as though we had been plunked down in an Ansel Adams photograph. The Sierra Nevada mountain range towered over Lake Tahoe and wrapped its crystal clear blue waters into a rough and beautiful embrace. I had read about Lake Tahoe in Mark Twain's *Roughing It* but not even Twain's words could do justice to the lake's clarity and beauty.

The lake and the many communities that surround Lake Tahoe, including the well-known, posh community of Incline Village, sit at 6,500 feet above sea level. A friend who had lived at high altitude for a time told us that during the first month our bodies would go through some changes to accommodate the lesser amount of oxygen. The only physical changes we noticed were some light-headedness the first few days, an insatiable thirst and dry skin that constantly beckoned for moisturizer.

Unlike John, I hadn't grown up spending time in the wilderness hiking, camping and exploring the great outdoors. If there wasn't indoor plumbing and thick mattresses with warm, fluffy covers, my family didn't have much to do with it. And my new surroundings were exactly that, new and a little daunting, but exhilarating at the same time.

That first year we spent many spring and summer mornings peering at the still snow-covered mountain peaks from our outdoor breakfast table while we decided what adventure to embark on that particular day. I relied heavily on John's hiking and mountaineering skills, trusting he would keep me safe during our many outdoor adventures. He introduced me to things I never would have considered exploring on my own. We spent most of that year donning our hiking boots, harnessing the dogs to their leashes and setting off to explore the many beautiful mountain ranges that were now our backyard. Fields blanketed with wildflowers, gurgling rivers and alpine lakes were all no farther than a 30-minute walk or drive from our Swiss-style mountain chalet home.

The closest I had been to any of this was back in the Shenandoah National Park in Virginia when I decided to humor John and go for an overnight camping trip with him. I didn't want to seem like a wimp, so I fibbed to him.

"Of course I've been camping before," I told him.

I left out the fact that it had been Girl Scout camp and we hadn't been more than 20 minutes from civilization. We'd slept in cabins, not tents.

My lie fell apart when I woke him at 2:00 in the morning our first night out. I was convinced an animal had made its way into our tightly sealed tent and I wanted him to find it and get it out.

"There's nothing in here but us," he tried to explain to me in his patient, sleepy voice.

"There is," I insisted. "I keep feeling it running around down near my feet. Please, John, please get it out," I had begged him, nearing panic mode.

He fully woke from his sleep, searched all 16 square feet of the tent with a flashlight, and finally convinced me that any critters I may have felt or heard were definitely on the outside of our tent.

If a small critter on the outside of our sealed tent had concerned me three years previous, imagine my reaction when our nice, helpful new neighbor mentioned that it wasn't uncommon for brown bears and coyotes to meander through our new neighborhood perusing for food.

"Why would they be looking for food here?" I asked like the city slicker I was.

"Because people leave food scraps in their garbage and bears are smart enough to take advantage of a free lunch," the neighbor answered. "Your best bet is not to put your garbage out until Tuesday morning, right before the trash men pick it up."

I turned my puzzled face to John, looking for reassurance.

"We're not in the big city anymore, Lizzy," he said, "We're living in the animals' neighborhood now."

After this realization I poured over a book I had seen in John's collection for years, but had dismissed as needless information. In fact, I had wondered more than once why in the world he had it. It was called, *Bear Attacks*, and was written by Stephen Herrero, the world's leading authority on bear ecology, behavior and attacks on humans.

"If I'm going to live in bear country, I guess I had better understand bears," I told John when he inquired what I was doing.

Feeling somewhat armed with my new knowledge on how to act or react if in the company of a bear, John and I explored our new surroundings. Initially we took short, relatively easy hikes but as summer progressed and our skills and muscles improved we worked our way toward my first three-day backpacking trip.

There were miles upon miles of trails laid out like a maze through the National Forest land that surrounded our house. One of the first truly challenging hikes John and I took was a rigorous trek up the side of a mountain ridge near our home. By the time we reached the summit of the 8,500 foot peak we were tired but exhilarated by the breathtaking panoramic view of our neighborhood 2,000 feet below and Lake Tahoe in the distance. All the houses were shrouded by the 60-foot-high towering pine trees and it really felt as if we were a million miles away from civilization.

As we walked along the still snow-covered ridge we marveled at the huge, hundreds-of-years-old sugar pine trees towering over our heads. We stopped at a shimmering alpine lake and a nearby old gold miner's cottage beckoned us to pull up a tree stump and sit on the deck to enjoy our well-deserved lunch of trail mix and water. An hour later, when John announced it was time to head down, I was amazed at how quickly the time had passed. While I hated to leave the tranquil beauty of the calm, glass-like lake I promised to return again and again and again.

That summer, I also learned how to mountain bike (in the mountains), backpack, camp and whitewater raft. Most importantly, I learned to enjoy the previously unimaginable beauty of nature in which I now lived. With winter came the new experiences of downhill and cross-country skiing, as well as snowshoeing. One cannot explain the quiet that you experience when snowshoeing through a valley blanketed with newly fallen snow. It was hard to decide which I liked better in Lake Tahoe, winter or summer. What I did know, though, was that I had discovered an adventurous side of myself I hadn't realized existed.

◆　　　◆　　　◆

My new-found life came to a screeching halt our second year. It was April of 1998, exactly one year since we had moved to the mountains.

What was supposed to be a three-day camping trip to see the wildflowers and desolate beauty of Death Valley ended abruptly our first morning there. We had driven nine hours over paved highways and 15 m.p.h. bumpy dirt roads to get from home to our camping spot in Death Valley the day before. After we'd set up camp and had dinner, we settled into our camping chairs to ogle the nighttime desert sky. It was indescribably beautiful and we sat for hours staring at the stars which seemed brighter and larger than I'd ever seen them. When we finally retreated to our tent and snuggled into our sleeping bags, I was so content I forgot to worry about the critters.

We woke early the next morning to an already hot day and were happy to step out of our stuffy tent into the fresh air. After we walked the dogs John set me to work helping him prepare breakfast. I was starved and happy when we sat down to our meal of oatmeal, sausage and fruit.

About five bites into my meal I found myself running for the campground bathroom. Twenty minutes later there was a knock on the door.

"Liz, are you okay?" I heard John's voice from outside.

I made my way out of the bathroom, ashen faced and shaking.

"I don't know what's wrong. I've got diarrhea like crazy and I can't stop shaking."

John led me back to camp and tried to get me to drink some water. He was worried.

"You've got to stay really well hydrated out here. You're in the desert, and they call it Death Valley for a reason."

I listened to him as I took a few sips from the canteen. I handed it to him and was back on the run to the bathroom.

This time when I emerged we had both come to the same conclusion—we had to get me out of the desert before I became so dehydrated I ended up in the hospital. In between trips to and from the bathroom I sat sipping water while John dismantled our camp. Half an hour later, the Jeep was packed and we were ready for the trip back home—not even 20 hours since we'd arrived.

As we bumped along the rutted dirt road toward home I felt tired and scared.

"I'm sorry," I told John.

"I know," he replied quietly. "Do you think it was the shish kebab last night?"

"I don't know," I told him honestly. "I hope not. It's great camp-fire food. But, it is a possibility. I felt really overheated this morning when we woke up. Maybe that did it. Maybe I just got overheated. Maybe."

We had to make a few unplanned stops along our path out of Death Valley. There were no bathrooms for miles and any reservations I may have had about dropping trow in the wilderness were put aside due to the urgency with which I had to go. When we arrived in

Bishop, California, the first decent-sized town outside the valley, we stopped at a convenience store where I bought some Imodium and used the bathroom. By the time we reached home later that night I felt exhausted and with the Imodium still working I easily fell asleep for the night.

Like me, John was disappointed by our abbreviated trip but he was also concerned about my health. I was simply puzzled.

"What had caused my stomach to go off like that?" I wondered.

I had been known to have stomach cramps here and there since my childhood. But many unpleasant and invasive tests during my high school years had shown that my stomach and intestines were fine. The doctors insisted it was stress and told me I needed to learn to "calm down."

As the days passed and the Imodium wore off my stomach settled and life got back to normal. Neither of us thought much more about the incident until a month later. Two weeks before our departure date for an anniversary trip to one of our favorite Caribbean islands, another bout of diarrhea hit. This time the diarrhea would not quit. I was constantly in the bathroom, for not one, not two, but three days. The Imodium I took had little to no effect this time. Something similar had happened on our honeymoon trip to the same island a few years before and the more recent Death Valley incident now reentered both of our minds. While I was sick and confused, John was confused and frustrated.

By the third day he was clearly agitated.

"Elizabeth, what is going on with you? Why is it that every time we try to go away these days you get sick?"

"I don't know!" My defenses went up.

"Is it me? Do you not want to go away with me?"

"John."

"I'm serious. I'm really beginning to wonder."

"Well, you can stop," I told him tenderly. "I love you. And I love traveling with you. You know that."

It was true. I loved my husband dearly, and our time spent traveling together was particularly enjoyable to me. We are a couple who travel very well together. Additionally, I adored the island we were planning to visit.

John had introduced me to St. Barthelemy the first year we dated. On an island no bigger than four square miles there were twelve beautiful beaches to choose from, each with its own special characteristics. I had immediately fallen in love with the island's glorious coastline, French culture and tropical temperatures.

But best of all was the laid-back island attitude. Being near an ocean always seemed to provide me with a sense of rejuvenation and calm that made me feel comfortable and creative. I delight in the salty air that fills my nostrils, the moist warm breezes brushing over my skin and the warm rays of sun deeply penetrating my entire being. John and I truly revealed our inner selves to each other on our first trip to this island. And it has remained a special place for both of us ever since.

Now, all I could ask myself was, "Why is my stomach doing this? And how do I make it stop?"

I decided it must be a bug. With memories of the invasive and unpleasant gastrointestinal tests from my high school years still in the back of my mind, I decided to see a local homeopath I had heard about from a neighbor. I hoped he would be less invasive in his procedures than a gastroenterologist would be. A gentle, quiet looking man, perhaps fifteen years my senior, the homeopath poked and prodded my abdomen and asked me question after question after question. Finally, he hypothesized that I had probably picked up a bug from one of our hiking experiences.

"Maybe from some stream water you drank," he said.

I thought it highly unlikely. We always took our own water or filtered any stream water we drank. But, I had no other explanations and guessed it could be possible.

He sent me home with an awful tasting pale yellow chalky liquid that was supposed to "clear it up."

It seemed to work.

By the day of our departure for St. Barth's my stomach had been okay for about a week. Our initial flight took us from Reno to San Francisco. During our two-hour layover at the airport we decided to grab some dinner. We both had chicken Caesar salads. We were then off to Philadelphia via the red-eye.

In Philadelphia we had an hour layover before our flight to St. Maarten where we would take a smaller airplane to St. Barth's. I went off to the ladies room to brush my teeth and freshen up while John headed for our departure gate. Instead of primping, I went directly to a bathroom stall. Suddenly, I had to go. Five minutes later I couldn't get off of the toilet. My stomach had let loose again. Ten minutes later I was still in the ladies room. I began to panic, which only made things worse.

"Why is this happening to me?" I said out loud to myself.

"You okay over there?" I heard a woman from the next stall ask.

"Yes, I'm fine," I answered, embarrassed at being overheard.

But I wasn't.

I finally made it to our gate where John was waiting for me. I had barely enough time to tell him what had happened before I was back on the run to the restroom. In between bouts of diarrhea I met John back at the gate and tried to gauge if I could continue our travels to St. Maarten. I was torn. I didn't know what was causing this, nor what to do about it. I wanted, more than anything, to go to St. Barth's with my husband, but I felt tired, achy, and incapable of controlling my gut.

I couldn't stay out of the bathroom for more than five or ten minutes at a time. How was I going to make it on a six-hour airplane flight with only four bathrooms for more than 200 people? I simply didn't know if I could go on.

John was visibly irritated, but tried to check his frustration.

On my fourth trip back to the gate he said, "Our plane is boarding and we have to decide right now if we stay or go. The decision is up to you."

"We should go, I'll be fine."

We gathered our carry-on luggage and made our way to the boarding line. As we got in line John handed me my boarding pass. I took it. Minutes later I handed it back to him and bolted for the bathroom again. When I returned, John was at the ticket counter. The agent wanted to know what we were going to do.

I stood there looking at the line of passengers dressed in shorts, sandals, and floppy beach hats boarding our plane. More than anything I wanted to be one of them.

"I don't think I can do it," I said reluctantly.

"Okay. Here are your tickets. You can try to re-book when you feel better," the agent said as she slid our tickets back across the counter toward us.

I shoved the tickets back toward her.

"No, I'm fine. We'll go."

"Are you sure?" she and John asked in unison.

"Yes!" I yelled at them in frustration, bolting for the restroom again.

This time as I emerged, John was waiting outside the exit.

"We'll spend the night here and see how you feel in the morning."

I felt relieved to have a decision made. I didn't have any more energy left. But I also felt terrible that we might have to cancel our trip.

"I think I need to find some Imodium," I whispered.

"Fine. You go find whatever it is you need to pull yourself together. I'll be checking us into the airport Hilton."

"John?"

"What?!"

All I could say before I had to find another ladies room was, "I'm really sorry."

"I just wish you had figured this out before we left," he said to my back.

◆   ◆   ◆

I was exhausted. I'd never been able to sleep on an airplane, so the combination of the all-night flight from San Francisco and the numerous bouts of diarrhea had completely wiped me out.

While I slept in our room at the Philadelphia airport Hilton John went to the American Airlines ticket counter to rebook our flights. It was not an easy task. There were no direct flights to St. Barth's for the next three days. We would have to fly to Puerto Rico instead, where we would spend our anniversary night before going onto St. Barth's the following morning.

While the Imodium had helped to quell the urgent rush of bathroom calls, I was afraid to risk infuriating my gut any further. I decided not to eat anything until we got to St. Barth's.

◆   ◆   ◆

Our anniversary night in Puerto Rico was not ideal. The Imodium had continued to keep me pretty stopped-up during our flight from Philadelphia, but I was still weak and tired from the diarrhea the day before and from not eating much since.

The warmer air and finally being outside the fifty contiguous United States seemed to buoy John's spirits. After we checked into our small and somewhat dirty hotel room he convinced me to take a taxi ride through the old part of San Juan. He had spent some time in the area on a string of business trips many years before, and was eager to show it to me.

He sensed my hesitation at spending the night out on the town and away from a bathroom.

"We won't even get out of the cab. I just want to show you the old part of the city. Then we'll come back to the hotel and we can go to sleep."

The town was beautiful and I wished I had felt better so we could take part in the city's bustling night life.

I slept well that night, and even though hunger pangs rumbled in my gut the next morning I was ready to make the last part of our journey. As we stepped from the nicely air conditioned hotel lobby into the steamy, hot, humid air of San Juan my breath caught in my throat. My skin immediately became moist with perspiration and I was sapped of the energy I had felt just moments earlier.

The breeze blowing through the open windows of the unair-conditioned cab as we made our way back to the airport cooled my skin and I seemed to regain some of my energy by the time we reached the airport terminal. Neither of us was sure where to find the counter for the small airline that we were now using, so John went off to search. I opted to stay with our luggage at curbside, thinking that the fresh air would do me some good.

Unfortunately, the now oppressive heat, mingled with the acrid stench of exhaust and cigarette smoke, drained the remaining ounces of energy from my body. I had been standing on the sidewalk with our luggage for only 15 minutes. It seemed like an hour.

I suddenly felt lightheaded and dizzy. I became aware of the emptiness in my stomach and felt like I could faint at any moment. I had to get inside the airport terminal, where I imagined it to be cooler. With my head reeling, panic began to wash over me. I tried to gather my thoughts and figure out how to get me and our four pieces of luggage into the terminal when John suddenly reappeared.

"You okay?"

"I don't think so. I feel like I'm going to keel over."

He grabbed our luggage.

"Let's get you out of this heat. It's air conditioned in the terminal. You'll feel better inside."

Once inside I plopped down on the nearest bench. Again, I waited with the luggage while John continued to try to locate the correct airline counter. By the time he came back I was feeling a bit better.

Loaded with our luggage, together we made our way through the terminal to our airline's ticket counter.

As we waited our turn in line I began to shake uncontrollably. I felt so weak and faint I dropped my bags, made my way over to a nearby wall and slowly slid down to the floor.

As he moved forward in line, John realized I was no longer behind him. He came over and knelt in front of me.

"What's wrong?"

"I don't know," I told him, scared and in tears. "I just don't know."

A well-dressed, olive skinned woman in her late 30's volunteered her opinion. "She looks like she needs some electrolytes."

John seemed slightly annoyed by the intrusion. "Excuse me?" he said to the woman.

"I am a doctor," she explained in an Argentinean accent, "She may be low in electrolytes. Gatorade might help."

A very handsome, tanned, French gentleman dressed in an airline uniform joined us from behind the ticket counter. He introduced himself as Jacques. We later found out he was the pilot who would fly us to St. Barth's.

"Come with me," Jacques said to John, "She is in good hands with the doctor. We will go find her something to drink."

John bent over and kissed the top of my head. "We'll be right back."

As he disappeared around the corner with the pilot I felt scared and alone.

As I sat there I tried to calm down. It was hard because I just didn't understand what was going on.

I went over all the fears in my mind.

What if I faint? What if my gut erupts again? What if I end up in a hospital in San Juan? We've already missed celebrating our anniversary on St. Barth's. I don't want to spend the rest of our trip in a Puerto Rican hospital.

John and Jacques reappeared.

John unscrewed the top from a bottle of juice and handed it to me. "We couldn't find any Gatorade, but we did find cranberry juice."

"That will be okay," the doctor said, "But Gatorade would be best."

"I don't think I can do this," I said. I was scared to put anything into my body for fear of what would then come out!

"Take small sips," the Argentinean doctor advised.

I took a sip. The sugary liquid felt good on my parched tongue.

"What I mean is, I don't think I can go onto St. Barth's," I said to John.

Jacques, the handsome French pilot answered.

"Of course you can. I am off to find a wheelchair for you and then we will get you onto the airplane."

"But what if something happens?!" I protested.

Jacques' French accent and piercing blue eyes transfixed me.

"What are you afraid of?" he asked.

I was too embarrassed to admit to him the real fear of losing control of my bowels in public. "Well…What if I faint?" I answered instead.

"Then we will get you to the island and find a doctor. It is not a problem," he said in a reassuring way. "If you are going to be sick, would you rather be sick here, or in St. Barth's?"

Without really giving me much of a choice, Jacques headed off around the corner.

Five minutes later he returned, pushing a wheelchair. It seemed ridiculous and unnecessary until I tried to stand up. I was now so weak my knees wobbled and I fell back to the ground.

John and Jacques both raced to my aid. They eased me into the wheelchair. Then Jacques wheeled me through the terminal and out onto the tarmac. There was no time to protest.

A small eight-passenger airplane sat in front of me waiting to whisk us over the ocean to the Caribbean island I love so much.

There was only one problem—no toilet.

I grew up flying on small aircraft like this and I knew there were no bathroom facilities aboard. My stomach did a flip-flop at the realization.

"You sit here so I can keep my eye on you," Jacques said as he guided me into the seat behind the co-pilot. "And if at any point during the flight you don't feel well you just let me know. Okay?"

I was still scared but glad to finally be on the airplane.

"Okay."

John, the doctor, her husband and three other passengers, who looked at me as if I had the plague, settled themselves into their seats.

My stomach did another quick flip-flop as the small aircraft took off, but the view of the azure blue ocean beneath us occupied my attention for the 45-minute flight to St. Barth's. By the time Jacques had landed our plane at the small island airport I was beginning to feel a little bit better.

"She should be okay," the Argentinean doctor counseled John. "Make sure she only eats bland food for a few days, and drink only bottled water while you are on the island. If she is not significantly better in a couple of days she will need to see a doctor." She handed John a piece of paper. "Here is the name and phone number of a friend of mine on the island. He is a doctor and you should call him if you need to."

I held out my hand to her. "Thank you. Thank you so much for all of your help. I don't think we would have gotten here without you and Jacques."

As we finished our good-bye with the doctor and her husband, Jacques waved to us as he settled himself onto the seat of a motorcycle then zoomed off toward the island's city center.

◆   ◆   ◆

For the first few days on the island I was so tired and weak I barely made it past the deck of our bungalow. This wasn't too awful because we had a spectacular sweeping view of the beach and Caribbean ocean below.

I didn't yet feel like going out to eat so John made daily trips to the French market down the street to stock up on the freshly baked crusty French baguettes we loved so much, as well as Camembert cheese, yogurt, pasta, and fish. Other than his grocery trips, John didn't leave the bungalow for three days. By our fourth day I began to regain my strength. The warmth of the sun rejuvenated me more than the yogurt and bread. We began venturing out, spending our afternoons lazing on one of the island's beaches. During one of our outings, a string-bikini-clad figure asked how I was feeling. After blocking the sun with my hand, I recognized the Argentinean doctor.

"Fine, thank you. I'm feeling much better," I told her. "The sun seems to agree with me."

"How can it not?" she agreed.

The next ten days of our trip were wonderful. We spent long, lazy mornings dallying over breakfasts of fresh bread, creamy French yogurt, and farm-fresh eggs. In the afternoon we often meandered through neighborhoods snapping photos of the unique island architecture, snorkeling in calm coves of warm salt water or lazing in the sugar-fine sand that stuck to our bodies as soon as we touched it. Evenings were for lingering over dinners of fresh fish, lobster and bottles of fruity, dry Merlot, topped off with starlit nights making love on the cabana's veranda. We were finally in the pure heaven I had remembered.

On our second to last night on the island, our heaven collided with hell. My gut let loose once again. We were forced to rush out of a restaurant before finishing our desserts. Their only bathroom was out of order and I estimated I had about five minutes, maximum, to find another one. An ice cream shop was open down the street and thankfully their bathroom was operational.

When we returned to our bungalow I spent nearly an hour in the bathroom. When I finally exited I saw the fury in John's face.

"What is wrong with you?" he demanded. "Why can't we just go on a trip without this happening?"

I broke into tears.

"I don't know. It's just as frustrating to me as it is to you. I don't understand what's going on either. I wish I did. But I don't."

"Well you better figure it out because I won't do this anymore. I feel like you don't want to be with me, and when you are, it makes you sick."

"John, that's not it and you know it. I love you."

By this time he had settled himself into the second bed in our bungalow's bedroom. It was obvious I would spend the night alone in our bed, or, more likely in the bathroom, where I headed once again. When I emerged the second time, John was already asleep in his own bed. I spent the night alone reading a Mary Higgins Clark novel I'd found in the bungalow's nightstand and making my way back and forth to the bathroom. Around sunrise I finally dozed off.

The next day was our last. Our flight was scheduled to leave the island at 1:00 that afternoon. While John sat on our veranda overlooking the Caribbean eating his breakfast, I packed my suitcase in between trips to the bathroom. My gut seemed calmer than the previous evening, but I was nervous about our impending trip.

As I moved between the bathroom and my suitcase I heard John's voice from around the corner.

"I don't understand why this happens."

I stepped out onto the veranda to face him. "Pardon?"

"I don't understand why this is happening. This never happened when we were dating, only now that we're married."

I was both frustrated and hurt by his comment. "What's your point?"

"My point is that you have to figure out why you are making yourself sick. Is it me? Is it us? What is it?!"

"I don't think I'm making this happen at all. In fact, I don't know why this is happening. I'm probably more frustrated and confused about it than you are."

"Well, maybe you are. But all I know is that I don't want to do this again. I don't want to live like this."

I wasn't quite sure where he was going with this conversation.

He got up and went to the sink to clean his coffee cup and bread plate. I stood in the doorway of the bedroom and waited. He finished drying his dishes then turned to face me.

"You have to figure this out, or I don't think I'll be around to be a part of it anymore."

I was stunned. Hearing his words scared me to death. Here was the man I loved convinced that I didn't want to be alone with him and threatening to leave our marriage because of it. He was wrong. I didn't know why I was always getting sick lately, but in my heart I knew that what was going on with my stomach didn't have anything to do with him, my feelings for him or our marriage.

Tears welled in my eyes. "I understand your frustration. But you're wrong about this. I know you are. If you'll just help get me home I'll do anything it takes to figure this out. Just give me six months to do it."

"Fine," he answered in a simple, curt tone I'd never heard him use before.

The airplane trip home was better than our trip to St. Barth's, but it was not without its challenges. While John helped me with my bags and checked us onto our flights, it was obvious from his continued silence that I was pretty much on my own for the rest of the trip home. He was hurt and confused and had withdrawn into himself, spending the majority of our travel time with his nose buried inside a book.

I prayed that the three Imodium capsules I had taken before we left the island would continue to dam up the floodgates within my bowels. Unfortunately, as soon as I was situated in my seat on the second leg of our trip, I felt the rumble in my gut that was becoming all too familiar. I made a beeline for the lavatory in the first class cabin. Five minutes later, as I emerged from the restroom scarfing down another Imodium, the first class cabin flight attendant was waiting for me. I expected a reprimand since my seat was in coach. To my relief she only asked if I was okay.

"I don't think so," I confided. "I've been having a severe stomach problem for about a week now and I just need to get home to figure it out."

She seemed genuinely concerned. "That's awful. Could it be an intestinal bug?"

"I don't know." Tears welled in my eyes again. "If I have a problem during the flight would it be okay if I come up here? I'm just in row 8."

She handed me a tissue. "Of course. Don't you worry. If you need the lavatory and someone is in there we'll clear them out for you just as quickly as possible."

For the first time in two days I mustered a slight smile. "Thank you very much."

As I headed back to my seat for takeoff I felt a little more confident about the rest of the trip home. I wished I felt confident about the rest of my life. Something was wrong with me. Really wrong. And I had six months to figure it out and save my marriage.

Tips and Information

- *Approximately 125 million Americans currently suffer with chronic illness. By 2020 this number could exceed 157 million.*

- *Medical costs for treating chronic illness in America will reach $1 trillion by the year 2020.*

- *Do not let your health problem go untreated until it hits a critical state.*

- *Learn to put your health ahead of others' needs. You can't have healthy relationships if you aren't a healthy person.*

- **www.healingwell.com** *is a website focusing on diseases, disorders and chronic illness.*

- **www.pbs.org/fredfriendly/who cares/***is a website devoted to chronic illness.*

3

Experimenting

We successfully made it home, and two days later I was back in the homeopathic doctor's office. Tears streamed down my face as I explained the events of the past two weeks.

"I don't understand what's happening to me. It's not stress like everybody thinks. I know stress, and this is not stress. Maybe it's the altitude," I continued babbling, "or the water. Could it be something in the water? I'm absolutely stumped as to what is causing this. But I do know that I have to figure this out or I'm afraid my husband will give up on me and leave."

My hands shook with the fear I'd been holding inside the past two weeks. Tears continued to trickle down my face. I was now so exhausted, I felt I could collapse at any moment.

"Elizabeth, listen to me," the doctor said. "I'll try my best to help you figure this out. But it could take us some time, as well as some trial and error. The first thing though, is that you need to calm down. Take a few deep breaths and try to focus with me on what we're going to do."

I breathed deeply, wiped away the tears, and waited to hear what he had to say.

"First, we'll need to get a stool sample to see if there is perhaps a parasite that is causing your problems. Then, I'll have you go to the hospital to get your blood drawn so we can check your white and red blood cell counts.

"The next thing that I think could help is for you, and maybe even your husband, to see a psychologist. Just to help you deal with the fear and stress of not yet knowing what's wrong with you."

I had made a phone call to our health insurance company that morning to find out if psychologist or psychiatrist appointments were part of our plan. It turned out they would pay 50% of the costs as long as I used one of their participating physicians.

"I've already made an appointment for next week to see a psychologist. But I really don't think this is stress. I know everybody thinks it is, but I just know it's not. I am not doing this to myself!"

I had heard the stress theory since childhood and I knew it was bogus.

"I understand," he said, trying to keep me calm. "I agree. I don't think you are causing the physical symptoms, per se, but I do think you are so stressed right now that it could be a contributing factor to the severity of the problem. Stress is very powerful and can make a physical problem worse. I think a psychologist could help you to learn how to manage your current stressful feelings."

"Whatever it takes, I don't have a choice anymore. I'll do anything to make this stop."

"That's good, Elizabeth. But you should understand that you do have a choice. In fact, you are the only one who does, because it's your health."

He paused to let this sink in.

"You can either keep going on the way you are, or you can decide to take control and try some other options to help yourself. But in the end it is your choice."

"I guess the fact that I'm sitting here asking you to help me tells me that I've already made my decision."

"Great. Now, the next thing I think you need to do is to go on an elimination diet."

The name alone scared me. "An elimination diet? What's that?"

"It cuts out all sources of sugar, wheat, and dairy from your diet for four weeks to cleanse your body of them. Then slowly, one product at a time, you will reintegrate those foods back into your diet. Your body's reaction to each food will tell us if you have any food allergies that could be causing your problems."

"But can't you determine food allergies through a blood test?" I asked.

The thought of a diet without wheat, sugar or dairy products sounded neither easy nor fun.

"Some doctors think so, but the blood tests are not completely reliable for determining food allergies. This diet is the best way to find out if you have food allergies or sensitivities."

The homeopath handed me two pieces of paper.

"Here's a list of the things you will be able to eat. If it's not on the list, don't eat it.

I must have looked shocked as I scanned the list.

He put a reassuring hand on my knee.

"I know the diet is restrictive and it will probably be hard to get used to for the first week or two. You are really going to have to pay attention to what you put into your body, and you'll have to relearn your cooking habits, shopping habits and eating habits, at least for the time being. But if it is a food allergy, you'll probably start to feel better within the first two weeks and you will get to a point where you won't want to change back to the diet that's been making you so sick."

"If this is what it's going to take, then I have to do it," I agreed. "But, if it is a food allergy, then why would it only be popping up now? Why wouldn't it have been present when I was born, or ten years ago?"

"Just as we can grow out of an allergy, we can also acquire an allergy. Environmental and geographical changes can all play a part in allergies, as well as the natural changes that our bodies go through as we age."

While I wasn't 100% convinced this was the answer to my problems it was a place to begin. And I was committed to figuring out what was wrong with me. I had to. Not only for me, but for my relationship with John, too.

◆   ◆   ◆

Even though we had been home from St. Barth's for two days, John had continued to be distant and withdrawn. Earlier that morning I had mentioned to John that I had a doctor's appointment that afternoon.

"Good for you," he'd responded in his curt voice again.

On the way home from my appointment I felt somewhat better. I had something definitive to do that might help me. On the other hand, I was a little scared to go home. I had never experienced John in such a contrary mood and it made me feel scared and uncomfortable. As I neared home I decided it was up to me to make John understand that I was serious about getting to the bottom of what was wrong with me. But more importantly, that I was willing to do whatever it would take to get things back on track with us.

When I arrived home I immediately walked upstairs to John's office and asked if he had a minute to talk. He didn't answer me. But he did turn around in his chair to face me. I took this as a sign that he was at least willing to hear what I had to say.

"I saw the homeopath again this afternoon."

I then recounted for him the information I had gleaned from the doctor. I also let him know I had an appointment with a psychologist for the following week.

I can't stand having people angry or upset with me, but especially John. I took a chance and sat on his lap as I had done a hundred times before. I feared he might throw me off. Instead, he looked straight into my eyes.

I locked eyes with him. "I'll get to the bottom of this, John. I know this has been as terrible for you as it has for me. But I love you, you know that. And I don't want to lose you. I promise, I'll figure this out for both our sakes."

"I know you will."

His eyes softened with the love I had missed seeing the past few days.

"I know you will," he repeated. "All I really want is for you to feel better. I know I've been awful these past few days, and I'm sorry for that. I was scared and worried and I didn't know what to do for you."

I wrapped my arms around his neck, "I know."

We held each other like that for minute after minute after minute letting our fear, anger, and frustration with the past couple of months melt away.

Finally we disentangled our arms from each other and John looked me square in the eye again.

"So, let's see this food list."

I grabbed the list off the floor where I'd dropped it and we settled down at his office desk to inspect the list of acceptable foods for my upcoming elimination diet.

"This doesn't look like fun," he commented.

"I know."

◆　　　◆　　　◆

With my food list in hand, John and I headed off to the grocery store the next morning. As we walked through the store's entrance I felt as if I had entered a land of uncharted territory. No bread, no lunch meats, no chips, no cheese, no sour cream, no, no, no. The whole store seemed off limits!

Taking charge, John grabbed a shopping cart, took my hand and headed toward the meat department.

"Let's start with what we know you can eat," he suggested, grabbing packages of chicken breasts, pork chops, and salmon steaks.

"That all looks good," I offered.

Then we were off in search of fruits and vegetables. John added green beans, avocados, mushrooms, bell peppers, lettuce, grapes, apples and oranges to our cart.

I removed the peppers, lettuce, grapes, and oranges. "Nope," I told him. But I can have pears, carrots, and rutabagas."

"What do you do with a rutabaga?"

"I don't know," I replied as I put two into a plastic bag. "But I guess I'll have to find out."

"How about yogurt?" John asked from the dairy section.

"Only if I make it myself. That stuff is loaded with sugar and preservatives," I explained. "And, Nutra Sweet. Apparently that stuff can be bad for even the best stomachs."

"Hmmmm," I heard from the dairy section. "How about eggs?"

"Yep, eggs are on my list." I was relieved to have at least one comfort food.

We spent the next hour scrutinizing labels, referring to my list and either rejecting or accepting products based on their ingredients.

Taco shells? No. Cereal? No. Canned soup? No. Dried beans? Yes. Nuts? Yes, but not peanuts. Hot chocolate? No, because chocolate has caffeine. Cheese? No. Canned tuna? Yes, as long as it is packed in water. Deli meat? No. Bread? Muffins? Pudding? No. No. No. And on it went as we proceeded through the store.

By the time we got to the last supermarket aisle one thing had become clear. If it was pre-packaged, pre-made, or canned, it most definitely was not on my list. I wasn't even allowed ketchup, mayonnaise, or butter.

It seemed impossible, but I couldn't even buy a can of black beans because every can I picked up had something added—sugar, salt, or some sort of preservative. Out of curiosity John and I looked at virtually every canned bean, vegetable, and fruit. They all had something added.

"Why does everything have sugar in it?" I asked incredulously.

"Until today I didn't realize it did," John answered. "But more importantly, I can't figure out why it would."

The one area of the diet that didn't seem to be quite as restrictive was beverages. I would have to cut out all caffeine, but I figured I'd be okay with herbal tea and juices to help supplement and liven up the eight glasses of water I would have to drink each day.

"I'm going to get some juice." I said, leaving John in the now forbidden cereal aisle.

When he found me a few minutes later I could barely speak. I was exasperated and deflated.

"Even the fruit juice has added sugar. It's going to be hard enough living without bread or pasta or coffee, but now I can't even find juice that fits this stupid diet."

"Are you sure it all has sugar in it?" John asked, trying to be helpful.

I snapped.

"I think I know how to read a label."

"Okay. Let's go grab some orange juice, that's got to be natural."

"It is, but oranges aren't allowed."

He lovingly squeezed my hand. "Hmmm. This could be difficult. But we'll figure it out together."

◆   ◆   ◆

The doctor was right. The first few weeks of my new diet left a lot to be desired. Breakfast wasn't too bad with eggs and fruit. And even my dinners of fish, poultry, or pork weren't much different from what I usually ate. I imagined this could really be hell if I had been a fast-food junkie.

Mid-days were the hardest. While I ate my lunches of dry canned tuna on a rice cake with carrot sticks or apple slices on the side, John would be in another room munching on a turkey and Swiss cheese sandwich filled with fresh, crunchy lettuce, red, juicy tomatoes and Dijon mustard to help it all slide down. And the crunching sound from the tortilla chips he would eat was hell. I loved tortilla chips!

I quickly realized the old adage was right. You really don't appreciate what you have until it's gone.

A few days later while I choked down a snack of almond nut butter and rice cakes, John announced he had located a Trader Joe's food store just an hour and a half from our house.

"It's in Reno," he'd said happily. "Who knew?"

I wasn't really sure how finding this store was a good thing for me. I recalled him mentioning Trader Joe's when he lived in Pasadena a few years before we got married. He had raved about their unique cheese and wine selections. Now, both were on my "verboten" list.

"Joe's has a lot of products that are wheat-free, gluten-free, and dairy-free. I'd never mentioned it before, because it wasn't relevant. But now, it's exactly what our new diet calls for," John said excitedly. "We might as well go have a look."

And so we made plans to drive to Trader Joe's in Reno the next morning.

It should have been a simple thing to do.

It wasn't.

As John sat in the car in our driveway, I sat on the toilet eating Imodium, wondering how I was going to make a 90-minute car trip when I couldn't even get out of the bathroom.

"I don't think I can go," I yelled to him a few minutes later from the front doorstep.

He turned off the car engine and walked toward me. I was sure he would be angry. But, his usual mild mannered style was back.

"Let's go sit in the sun on the deck. It seemed to help calm your stomach in St. Barth's. If things calm down then we'll get going. If they don't, maybe we'll try again tomorrow."

I was relieved at how understanding he was. It was a big change from his reaction in St. Barth's. I, on the other hand, was frustrated and ticked off that I couldn't even leave the house to run a simple errand.

I settled into a deck chair and let the high alpine sun warm my body. The first year we lived at Lake Tahoe I had been surprised by the intensity of the sun at our 6,500-foot elevation. I was now glad for the thinner air and strong sunshine. After fifteen minutes of letting the sun's rays penetrate my body I actually felt my stomach grow calmer.

Thirty minutes later John and I were driving through Hope Valley toward Reno. In the time we had lived in Lake Tahoe, Hope Valley had quickly become one of my favorite places. The towering Sierra Nevada mountains part to make room for this beautiful, rambling expanse of land that seems to stretch forever. Tall, swaying Aspens interweave with the beautiful old towering pines, while thousands and thousands of wildflowers dapple miles of valley hills.

As we drove alongside the narrow, but powerful, Carson River that snakes through the valley, I wondered if I was going to need a bathroom stop.

I decided to try putting my mind on something else as we followed the river's twists and turns.

"This isn't 'our' diet," I told John. "You can eat anything you want. You and that steel drum stomach of yours. It's always amazing to me how you could eat wormy dirt, e-coli laced water and jalapeno peppers and not have an upset stomach afterwards."

"I know. I can't help it, though. Drinking the public water in Spain in the '60s while I was growing up made my system impervious to much of what causes other mere mortals severe gastrointestinal upset. And any way, it is 'our' diet," he said as we continued to wind our way through the beautiful river canyon. "I'm really proud of what you're doing. Plus, I know it's not easy, and I want to be supportive."

While I would have liked to relish in the support and love of my husband, all I could manage to say, was "Thanks, but what I really need right NOW is a bathroom!"

◆   ◆   ◆

In addition to Trader Joe's, we found a local health food store about five minutes from our house. The prices were high but I was able to buy wheat-free, gluten-free, and dairy-free products that I couldn't find anywhere else. The health food store even had fruit juice that was juice made from fruit!

I had let my adventurous side take over during the elimination period and tried eating sour cream and mayonnaise made from tofu. Initially, they both sounded awful to me. After I got used to their flavors I actually preferred them to the real McCoy.

These experiences also convinced me to experiment with some recipes I found in two cookbooks I bought boasting dairy-free and wheat-free recipes—*Breaking the Vicious Cycle* by Elaine Gottschall B.A., M.Sc. and *The Complete Food Allergy Cookbook* by Marilyn Gioannini.

My first attempt at gluten-free baking was to make kamut flour pancakes for breakfast one Sunday morning. They were oddly flat in comparison to the buttermilk blueberry pancakes I usually made.

"Not too bad," John said politely as he reached for more syrup to pour over his remaining pancakes.

I took my first bite and nearly gagged. They were awful, terrible, horrible things that were simply not fit for human consumption.

I cleared our plates off the table and flung the Frisbee-like pancakes into the garbage.

The soybean spread on rice crisps and honey-ginger chutney sauce over broiled chicken breasts went over much better.

When I explained some of the things I was eating to my family, one of my sisters joked that I was becoming a West coast granola-crunchy girl. While she was probably right, I was thankful for all of the products and information that were available in my California neighborhood. Had I been back on the East coast, or in the Midwest at this time I imagined my quest to find sources for wheat-free, gluten-free and dairy-free foods would have been much harder, if not virtually impossible. It wouldn't have been quite so socially acceptable, either. But in California I was verging on trendy!

In the years since 1998 when I embarked on this elimination diet, food allergies and sensitivities have become more understood and mainstream, meaning that wheat-free, gluten-free and dairy-free products are available in most mainstream grocery stores today. Health food stores are now in nearly every city and even Trader Joe's stores are inching their way throughout cities across the U.S.

For the next four weeks my life was consumed with following this new diet. I continued to research food allergies and sensitivities. I found more wheat-free, gluten-free, and dairy-free recipes through the Internet and even perfected an applesauce spelt muffin that was not only edible, but pretty darned good!

While I was doing well with all the changes, the diet was even harder than I had imagined and at times my food choices were just plain boring. But, I continued to follow the restrictions religiously. By the second week I started to feel a little bit better. I wasn't cured by any means but I found my energy level a little higher than it had been a couple of weeks earlier, and the diarrhea didn't seem quite as constant or painful as it had been the previous month. I was still losing weight though—at 5 feet 7 inches tall I had gone from my usual 118 pounds six months earlier to 106 pounds.

After the end of the fourth week of my new diet I was allowed to add one previously eliminated food every few days. The first item I chose to add was cheddar cheese. I really thought I would have missed bread, or cereal, or pasta more, but I found that I was craving cheese. So, I ate a portion of cheese three times a day for two days then continued on the elimination diet for two more days, monitoring how I felt both physically and emotionally. If I didn't notice any adverse changes or reactions I was then allowed to add one more previously eliminated item. This pattern continued until I had added back all the previously eliminated food groups.

The homeopath had also asked that I keep copious notes of everything during my elimination diet—how many bowel movements I had each day, what they looked like, their consistency, my mood, how my skin looked and felt, my energy level, weight and everything I ate, felt, or did.

I called these daily entries my "poop diary." I prayed that nobody else would ever find them. I mean, truly, what if I had been hit by a

Mack truck and as my family and friends went through my treasured belongings they came across my "poop diary?" What *would* they think as they read them?

July 14th, they would read, 8 bm's, loose, greenish-brown. Low energy level early morning, better after 2:00 p.m. Breakfast: 2 eggs, half a pear, rice cake. Lunch: Tuna on rice cake with tofu mayonnaise. Carrots. Snack: Almonds, 4 apple slices. Dinner: Broiled chicken breast, green beans, cauliflower. Terrible cramps 45 minutes after dinner, vile smelling diarrhea 60 minutes after dinner, stomach calmer by bedtime. Mild cramping continued throughout the night.

I kept my poop diary tucked between a year's worth of *Writer's Digest* magazines and a self-publishing manual on my office bookshelf hoping the doctor and I would be the only two people ever to read it.

By the end of my diet I found out that red meat, grapefruit, oranges, yellow corn, milk, caffeine (including chocolate), red food coloring, lettuce, raw vegetables, melon, preservatives, alcohol (especially beer) and anything spicy all sent my stomach into a tail spin, rendering me useless and in the bathroom for days.

Red meat, oranges, corn, milk and red food coloring I figured I could live without. But a staple of my diet had always been salad. I loved the fresh, crunchy taste. I thought lettuce would be a hard thing to give up. It proved easier to do once I realized that eating even a small salad would set my gut off for days.

Milk wouldn't be hard to give up because I enjoyed the soy milk that had been part of my new diet. Even John preferred the soy milk over cow's milk, and we had found a brand that was full of all the essential vitamins and nutrients that we would need. But, I did love ice cream and of course it's made with milk, so that was out. I decided I would have to try eating John's frozen yogurt instead. The taste wasn't as melt-in-your-mouth yummy as ice cream, but it might fill the void.

Caffeine would also be difficult to eradicate from my life. I was pretty much addicted to coffee and Coca-Cola and I had really been looking forward to being able to drink both beverages once I was off the diet. It was obvious though, that I was going to have to decide how important drinking a glass of Coke or having a cup of coffee was to me, versus possibly spending hours or days in the bathroom and feeling awful.

During the elimination process I had about a week's worth of caffeine withdrawal headaches. And in the end, the choice to give up Coke and coffee for my health wasn't a hard one to make. I actually realized later that what I liked so much from the Coke was the carbonation, which I figured I could get from sparkling water. As for coffee, I just learned to enjoy the smell of it. As John brewed his morning cup of java, I would steep a cup of peppermint tea. During my many hours of reading I found out that peppermint is good for digestion and soothing to the gut!

I would also find out through trial and error over the years that uncooked vegetables and fruit were very hard on my stomach. Vegetables like broccoli, green beans, asparagus, and avocados seemed to agree with my stomach the most. Later I would be able to add tomatoes, yellow and orange bell peppers, cucumber, and eggplant to the list. Bananas, pears, and any kind of berry—strawberry, blueberry, raspberry—proved agreeable to my system. But cantaloupe, oranges, and apples still remain on my "don't eat" list to this day.

I also realized with time that preservatives were an absolute killer on my gut. If a food included a word that I didn't understand, my rule became not to eat it. That meant that any kind of fast food was out, prepared foods were out and anything pre-packaged was out of my diet as well. It wasn't too hard for me to get used to these changes because I had never been a fast food junkie, nor did I buy a lot of premade or pre-packaged foods. But it did mean that I had to take a little more time to plan my meals before I went shopping and then spend a little more time preparing meals. In the end, I found the extra effort I put into preparing my meals to be worth the pay-off of feeling a little bit better. And, since John likes to cook, this has become an activity we do together.

Eating out or away from home could be a challenge. I now had to ask many questions of waiters and waitresses and select foods that were the least likely to have extra, added ingredients.

One evening when we were preparing dinner together John asked if I wanted a salad.

"No thank you. Lettuce is on my 'don't eat' list. Remember?"

"That's right. I wonder if the salad you ate in San Francisco when we were flying to St. Barth's was what set off your stomach?"

I was stunned at the connection. Could it have been that simple? Could a salad really have been the cause of our nearly ruined honeymoon trip?

Maybe.

◆   ◆   ◆

A few months later, after I had completed my diet, the homeopath and I reconvened. I shared my results with him, including my poop diary. He seemed pleased to hear about the progress I had made and reiterated what I had already realized about not eating prepared foods because they are made with preservatives.

"Your best bet will be to eat foods in their natural state," he suggested. "Shop in the outside aisles of the grocery store where the fruits, vegetables, and meats are located. Traveling down the inside aisles can get you into trouble."

This was nothing I hadn't already learned in the past months, but it was a good reminder.

I expected our appointment to end there. He, however, had a new concern.

"Your stool tests came back negative," he told me, "And that's good because at least we know we aren't dealing with a parasite. However, your blood tests show that you are pretty low in some vital vitamins."

"Can that affect my gut?"

"Yes, sometimes. I'd like to get you taking Vitamins C, B12 and B6 to start."

He told me the doses he wanted me to take, which seemed high since I hadn't taken a vitamin in months. I asked him whether I shouldn't start with lower doses and increase them over time.

"You should be fine," he reassured me. "I've got a number of other patients with stomach and food sensitivity problems taking these dosages and we've seen real improvement."

I'd never been a big vitamin taker, maybe a multi-vitamin here and there, but nothing else. Based on his medical knowledge and say-so I agreed and went home laden with my new vitamin bottles.

Within two days of taking my new vitamin cocktail I had the worst diarrhea I had ever experienced. I could barely leave the bathroom for two days. By the night of the second day I was exhausted and extremely sick again. My body shook uncontrollably for hours, and my muscles ached. When the diarrhea hadn't stopped by 3:00 a.m. I got scared that something was seriously wrong.

John had been dubious about the vitamins from the beginning. Now he was convinced they were the cause of my current stomach problem. He wasn't exactly sure why I was shaking, but it was reminiscent of our St. Barth's experience. He forced me to drink small sips of Gatorade. We now kept a bottle or two in the house at all times. Just in case.

I had never had any episode of diarrhea this severe in the past. I was beyond the point of being able to care for myself so I followed John's instructions. As the night wore on, the shaking and bathroom visits lessened and finally we were both able to get a couple hours of sleep.

The next morning I telephoned the doctor.

"I've never heard of anybody reacting like that to the vitamins and dosages I gave you," he told me. "It may just take your system a day or two to get used to the increased vitamin levels."

I was incredulous.

"You think I should continue to take them?" I asked.

"Yes. Cut the Vitamin C dosage in half for a few days, and then try taking the whole dose again by the end of the week."

Something about what he was telling me to do just didn't sound right. I wanted to stick with him, but after doing some further research on the Internet and with the staff at my local health food store I found out that taking too much of specific vitamins can cause problems for people with certain illnesses. I decided to stop taking all of the vitamins for the time being.

The information I had read concerned and frightened me. While the homeopathic doctor had helped identify my trigger foods, I now felt I needed to look into other options to further pinpoint my problem. I decided it was time to call my parents in Wisconsin. They gave me the name and phone number of the gastroenterologist I had seen when I was 15. He, in turn, gave me the name of one of his colleagues in Reno.

His name is Dennis Yamamoto. My Wisconsin doctor said he was top in his field and located nearby in Reno. All well and good I thought, but still, a gastroenterologist who would want to do every type of invasive test on me known to his field.

As I sat with Dr. Yamamoto's office phone number in one hand and the telephone in the other, I thought about my options. I had found out some really good, helpful information from my elimination diet. Except for the vitamin problem, my gut seemed a little bit better than a couple of months ago. But, I was still losing weight. I now weighed only 102 pounds. The stomach cramps had worsened again during the past month and even with my modified diet I wasn't anywhere near back to normal.

I truly believed I had done what I could on my own, but knew I had to explore everything and anything to dig to the bottom of what was causing my body to virtually reject itself.

I punched the cordless telephone's "Talk" button and dialed Dr. Yamamoto's office.

"Hi," I said to the receptionist, "My name is Elizabeth Roberts and I need to see the doctor as soon as possible."

Tips and Information

- **Homeopathic medicine** *is a natural pharmaceutical science that uses various plants and minerals in small doses to stimulate a sick person's natural defenses.*

- ***www.homeopathic.org***—*the National Center for Homeopathy website.*

- *The* **Elimination Diet** *removes those foods from your diet that most often cause problems—gluten, wheat, dairy, citrus, corn and nuts.*

- *Gluten-free, wheat-free and dairy-free resources include:*

  Breaking the Vicious Cycle by Elaine Gottschall B.A., M.Sc.

  The Complete Food Allergy Cookbook by Marilyn Gioannini

  www.foodallergy.org—*The Food Allergy & Anaphylaxis Network provides information on food allergies and recipes.*

  www.glutenfree.com—*The Gluten-Free Pantry provides information and gluten-, wheat-, and dairy-free products for purchase.*

  www.gluten-freemall.com—*features products for gluten-, wheat-, and dairy-free diets.*

  www.allorganiclinks.com—*links to companies offering organic products.*

  www.pacificbakery.com—*sells dairy-, egg-, sugar-, yeast-, and wheat-free products.*

- *Dr. Kenneth Fine's website*—**http://finerhealth.com**—*is a good resource for people with microscopic colitis and gluten sensitivity or celiac disease.*

4

Finding Answers

"Are you here to see the doctor?"

I was already nervous as I sat in the waiting room of the gastroenterologist's office. But when an older gentleman walked by us leaning on a metal walker that had a bunch of medicine bags hanging from a hook attached to one of its handles I almost bolted for the door.

He was speaking to my husband.

"Yes," John answered. "My wife is here to see Dr. Yamamoto."

As I stared at all the tubes leading from the man's walker and snaking their way under his shirt I wondered what was wrong with him. Would I end up like that some day?

Our drive to Reno had been terrible. I had taken two Imodium before we ever left the house, but we still had to visit virtually every restroom along the 90-mile route. We were now late for my appointment. I sat, rudely staring at the old man, knowing that I shouldn't, and waited in dreaded anticipation of meeting Dr. Yamamoto.

I mustered a brief smile when the older gentleman caught me staring. "You're in good hands," he told me. "Dr. Yamamoto is the best."

I felt rescued when the nurse called my name. I virtually ran toward her to get away from the sickly man.

◆   ◆   ◆

I stepped on the scale the nurse pointed out to me. I had opted to leave on my shoes, sweater and purse. But still the scale registered that I'd lost another two pounds, bringing me down to a record low weight of 100 pounds! I also found out my blood pressure was abnormally low. When the nurse finished taking my vitals I asked for directions to the nearest bathroom.

As I walked from the bathroom back to my examination room, a short, pleasant looking Asian man walked up beside me and introduced himself as Dr. Dennis Yamamoto.

He's not scary looking at all, I thought to myself.

In fact, he had a nice, soft voice and a large winning smile. My fears seemed to subside, if only just a little bit.

The doctor and I settled back into my examination room where I gave him the history of my past six months. I started with our Death Valley trip and ended with my elimination diet results and the vitamin escapade.

"So, it seems that it would be wise to discontinue taking those vitamins for the time being," he said as he examined my abdomen.

"Your stomach is awfully grumbly," he commented as he removed his stethoscope from his ears.

"I opted not to eat this morning to make it easier to get here."

He took my hand to help me sit up on the end of the exam table. "Why don't you come down and make yourself comfortable so we can talk some more."

I stood up, tucked my shirt into my size 2 pants and settled into a chair across from the doctor.

"Is there any family history of stomach problems?"

"My father has ulcerative colitis, and my mother has irritable bowel syndrome."

"And the past six months is the first time you've ever had a stomach problem?"

"No. I had problems in high school. They did upper GIs and lower GIs, then told me that it was just stress and I should learn to calm down."

"So between high school and the past six months you haven't had any other gastrointestinal problems or episodes like this?"

I didn't answer for a few beats as I thought. I'd been so wrapped up in my current problems that I hadn't really considered my past history.

"Not exactly," I replied slowly. "I did have a lot of stomach cramps in college for a while. They gave me Compazine until I had a bad reaction to it, so they gave me Tagamet instead. It seemed to help."

"And that's it?" he asked.

I paused to think further.

"Noooo, I don't think so."

This was the first time I had been asked about specific events related to sudden bouts of diarrhea. It was amazing how many incidents I was now able to recall when my stomach had just let loose. For the next 30 minutes I relayed each incident to this doctor, whom I suddenly trusted.

"My Mom said I was the kid who was always constipated," I told him. "But, if I'm remembering correctly, my first bout of diarrhea started on our honeymoon in May of 1996. We were on our favorite Caribbean island and we'd had a great dinner of lobster, with wine and Grappa, a rum-vanilla flavored after-dinner drink. We also had some champagne that was left in our bungalow by our hosts. We had had a wonderful first evening of our honeymoon until I woke up about 3:00 in the morning and could barely get to the bathroom fast enough. I spent the rest of the night in there with terrible diarrhea. I finally made it back to bed around 6:00 a.m. and woke John to tell him that I was really ill."

Dr. Yamamoto wrote some more notes in my chart.

"Probably not the way you wanted to spend the first night of your honeymoon."

"Not really. Anyway, we both figured it was just a stomach upset from the water and figured I'd be fine by the end of the day. But it went on through that day, that night and into the next day and night. On the third day John took me down to the local pharmacy. Through John's rudimentary French and a lot of hand signals we were finally able to help the proprietress understand my problem. The fact that I looked like death probably helped too. She gave me some capsules to take twice a day and told me to eat yogurt. We later found out that the capsules were acidophilus."

The doctor nodded, and motioned for me to continue.

"I finally slept through that night and the next day I was able to leave our bungalow. I was very weak and had to be careful what I ate for the next few days, but I felt fine by our second week on the island. We pretty much chalked it up to a stomach bug."

"Some bug," Dr. Yamamoto joked. "So that's it?"

"Well, no."

I remembered an evening in Washington, D.C. in the fall of 1996. John and I had gone to a reception at the British Embassy. We had a few gin and tonics and appetizers while we socialized. After the reception we went out to dinner and to a few jazz clubs in Old Town, Alexandria, Virginia. We had wine with dinner and I had another glass or two at the clubs. I felt buzzed, but nothing I hadn't felt before. Again, around 2:00 in the morning I woke up with terrible cramps and diarrhea. Again, I spent the night dozing on the bathroom floor in between bouts.

"It sounds like perhaps alcohol could be a trigger here," Dr. Yamamoto commented.

"Maybe, except that there have been plenty of times when I've had alcohol that this hasn't happened. But maybe more importantly, there have been other episodes of diarrhea that haven't involved alcohol at all."

Episodes that I could readily recall at the time included our second house hunting trip to Lake Tahoe in February 1997, a trip to Prescott, Arizona in November of '97 and a trip to Southern California in early '98 to meet some of John's childhood friends. We'd had a nice dinner with them but our night was cut short when a bout of diarrhea hit minutes after getting back to our hotel. Unceremoniously, I shoved John and his friends out of our room while I headed to the toilet. I was sure they must have thought I was the rudest person in the world. Little did they know it would have been even ruder had I allowed them to stay. I also recalled a similar episode during a later trip to Southern California in November of 1998.

"Hmmm. Anything else you can think of that we haven't already discussed?"

"I did have a bout with pseudomembraneous colitis in 1993."

"Was it from an antibiotic?"

"Yes. Ceftin. But I didn't know what was going on at the time. I didn't really have diarrhea with that, just bloody stools and really awful cramps. I saw a gastroenterologist who did a sigmoidoscopy. He said everything looked fine."

"Okay. Anything else you can recall?"

I launched into our last European trip. We had gone to meet some of our British friends who were in Lake Thun, Switzerland in September of 1997. I had been fine our first week in the country. I had drunk the local Swiss wine and beer with the rest of our friends, eaten the local cheeses, sausages and bread and hadn't had any stomach-related troubles. Through a friend who had spent a good deal of time in the Lake Thun area of Switzerland, we had been invited to participate in a unique village festival called Justistaler.

The festival takes place in this particular Swiss region each fall when the local farmers take their herds of cows and goats from the high pastures to the lower pastures for winter. But it is also a time for the farmers and their families to celebrate the cows that provided the most milk for making cheese throughout the summer. While our group hiked to the mid-valley, the local farmers and their families rode their motorized flatbed tractors to the cheese houses located there. We later found out that the tractors were needed to carry the many 5, 10 and 15 kilo wheels of cheese that were to be divided among the farmers according to the amount of milk their herds had given over the summer months. This is called the dividing of the cheeses.

The day was filled with local farmers yodeling while others played the long, baritone Alp horn that I had only previously seen on Ricola television commercials. As had been typical of the previous week, we sampled the farmers' homemade cheeses, wines, breads and pickled vegetables. The most exciting and beautiful point in the whole day was to see the flower-bedecked herds of cattle come around the corner from the high ground to make their way down to their lower winter pastures. Each herd was headed up by that group's best milk-producing cow. To celebrate its accomplishment, each top producer was awarded with a beautiful flower headdress made of huge, colorful tissue-paper flowers. An even huger gleaming brass bell swayed below the cow's neck and boomed a low *clink, clink, clink,* as the large but gentle animals walked down the hill.

The day had been magical. We were rightfully tuckered out by the time we arrived back at our chalet that evening and we headed straight to bed. The magic was broken when I woke in the middle of the night with cramps and diarrhea. Another night was spent making my way from bed to bathroom in between bouts of diarrhea. The next day I was so tired and out of energy that we stayed at our chalet instead of hiking with our friends.

"Did that finally prompt you to stop drinking?" Dr. Yamamoto asked.

"I suppose for a while, but I still had a glass of wine with dinner here and there, or a gin and tonic, which has always been a favorite of mine. But I did find that beer just didn't appeal to me anymore. The smell made me nauseous, and if I drank it I felt really bloated afterward. Which was weird, because having gone to school in Milwaukee, I had drunk a lot of beer in my college years and had never had either of these problems before.

"Also, it wasn't as if every time I had a drop of alcohol I got diarrhea. In fact, I went along fine for the rest of that year without another problem until this past April. Without any alcoholic initiation, these terrible bouts of diarrhea just started. They could hit at anytime, but I've found that nighttime or first thing in the morning is when the episodes usually start. And if it hits in the morning, it lasts virtually all day and sometimes more than one."

I then added my experience with the homeopathic doctor, our terrible second trip to St. Barth's, and the results of my elimination diet.

"Interesting," he said in agreement, "And even somewhat helpful in treating your symptoms. But it still doesn't tell us why you are having these episodes of diarrhea. As evidenced by your dramatic weight loss, there is a problem. And I believe the best place for us to start looking for an answer is with a colonoscopy."

My heart felt like it had skipped a beat and my palms began to sweat as I clenched them tightly together in my lap. The doctor had just uttered the words that I feared the most. While I had never had a colonoscopy, I knew my father and my mother had, and I knew they were not particularly pleasant, no matter what Katie Couric had to say about them on national television. Unfortunately, I also knew I didn't have any alternatives.

◆   ◆   ◆

My colonoscopy took place a week later. The most awful and uncomfortable part of the entire procedure began the night before. Starting at 5:00 p.m., I was to drink one 8-oz. glass of a vile-salty-tasting solution every 20 minutes until an entire gallon of the concoction was gone.

The purpose of the solution is to completely clean out your intestinal tract so that the long, flexible colonoscope can make its way through the intestine while the doctor views your insides on a television screen. He also would be able to take pictures and biopsies of the colon along the way.

The biggest challenge I found in the preparation was being able to completely drink each 8-oz. glass of solution before I either threw it up or had to be in the bathroom again. The solution is tricky because it renders you absolutely without control over your bowels and you pretty much spend the next five to seven hours in the bathroom pooping out your insides.

I had been through a similar type of preparation once before in my high school years for a different test, so I had a vague idea of what to expect. I definitely knew I did not want my husband or my 14-year-old stepson, who was with us for his summer vacation, to be anywhere near the house for at least the next four hours.

With a kiss and a hug I sent them off to have dinner and see a movie, leaving me alone to inflict hell upon my body.

The next morning when I woke up I was shaking and drained of all energy. I had been instructed by Dr. Yamamoto's nurse not to eat anything after 5:00 p.m. the previous night and was allowed only small sips of water in the morning. The water went through my skeletal 100-pound body within minutes.

John drove me to my appointment in Reno, pausing at all of our usual bathroom stops along the way. It was amazing that there could be anything left inside of me!

"At least I know where all the clean bathrooms are between Tahoe and Reno," I joked to John after our third stop. "Maybe I should write a travel guide citing the best and worst of California and Nevada's public bathrooms."

It hadn't been such a crazy idea. A few years later on the Travel Channel, I actually watched a show that ranked the top-10 restaurant bathrooms in the world!

◆　　　◆　　　◆

The actual colonoscopy was easy. The anesthesia knocked me out moments after Dr. Yamamoto entered my testing room. When I woke up in the curtained-off recovery area it was all over. Dr. Yamamoto and John were both there.

"Her colon looked good," the doctor told my husband as I lolled in and out of consciousness. "I really don't expect the biopsy results to show anything different. But, we'll see her back here in a week when they're in."

An hour later the doctor's office released me and we were on our way home. I was still a little groggy from the drugs, but was glad it was all over. All I wanted now was to start feeling better. But, thirty minutes down the road I didn't feel so well.

"I think I'm going to throw up," I told John as I hung my head out the car window like a dog.

"Okay, I'll pull over up here."

It was too late. I had thrown up out the window as we drove down the main street of historic Carson City, Nevada.

"Well, that was pleasant," I said as I pushed the button to roll up the window.

"I'm not so sure those tourists thought so," he chuckled.

I hadn't even noticed the tourists. I honestly didn't care what they thought. I just wanted to get home. I felt awful.

The rest of my day was spent sleeping, sipping ginger ale and sucking on Jell-O cubes.

John spent the rest of that day packing and organizing for a business trip he had to make very early the next morning. The timing of the trip was anything but ideal, but it couldn't be postponed. He was meeting with Dan Quayle to discuss a job opening on Quayle's 2000 presidential election campaign. John knew Quayle from his days working in the Reagan-Bush White House and when Quayle's campaign manager had called a couple of weeks earlier to ask if John would be interested in working for them, we decided he should check it out.

With my health on the outs I wasn't able to work. Our income levels were vastly below what we had previously anticipated when we had left D.C. for Lake Tahoe so we both agreed that it couldn't hurt to see what the campaign was offering.

John's son, Ben, had been with us for a few weeks and was scheduled to fly back to Washington, D.C. the following day.

"Are you sure you'll be able to get Ben to the airport tomorrow?" John asked as I lay on our bed watching him pack. "Because he could just come with me in the morning and wait in the airport until his flight in the afternoon."

"No, I don't want him sitting around the airport alone for four hours," I told him. "I'll be fine. His flight isn't until noonish, and I'll feel a lot better by tomorrow."

I didn't.

John left at 5:00 a.m. and when I woke up at 8:00 a.m. I still felt like a skeleton—hip bones protruding, stomach hollow—but even more frightening than that was I felt how I imagined a starvation victim must feel. A terrible emptiness had settled into the pit of my stomach making me feel nauseous, light headed and with barely enough energy to stand upright. I dragged myself downstairs to the kitchen and forced myself to eat some yogurt. The smell of it made me even more nauseous, but I knew I had to eat something if I was going to get my energy back.

It didn't work. I had swallowed only four bites before I threw up. I began to panic. How was I going to drive Ben 90 miles to the Reno airport when I could barely walk down the hall of my house and back upstairs? I couldn't get a hold of John. He was on an airplane that wouldn't land for another hour. Back upstairs I sat down in my office to think about my options.

"Liz, you okay?"

It was Ben. I really didn't want him to see me with tears running down my cheeks. But I couldn't even muster enough energy to put on a brave face for him.

"I don't think so," I told him. "I'm still really weak from my test yesterday and I don't seem to be able to eat anything to help restore my energy. I'm trying to figure out how I'm going to get you to the airport."

"Sorry you don't feel well. Can I do anything for you?"

He had to be the most caring and polite kid I had met in a long time. At that particular moment I felt very fortunate to have him as my stepson.

"Thanks, Ben. I think I'm going to call a friend and see if she can drive you to the airport this morning. Why don't you go get showered and make sure you have all of your things together and packed?"

"I can wait until tomorrow," he offered. "Maybe you'll feel better by then."

"Maybe, but I think we should try to get you on today's plane. The routes are pretty booked up and your Mom has plans for you tomorrow."

"Oh yeah," he replied, padding off to the bathroom.

I called my friend.

"Of course I can take him," she said. "All I need is some money for parking and a promise from you that you'll take care of yourself."

◆　　　◆　　　◆

It took a week for me to regain my appetite. I now weighed 98 pounds. The test had set me back another two pounds. I looked disgusting, I felt terrible and I still spent much of my time in the bathroom. My strength was still eluding me and it seemed I had little, if any, control over what was happening to me.

I remember emerging from the upstairs bathroom at one point, hunched over at the waist because that position seemed to lessen the severity of the abdominal pains that were now almost constantly present. John, who thankfully had returned from his trip, met me in the hallway and helped me back to the futon in our guest room. I'd taken up residence there because the futon was easier for me to get into and out of than our bed and it was nearer the bathroom.

"Is there anything I can do for you?" he asked, his voice full of concern.

"Honestly?"

He nodded.

"You could take me out back and shoot me."

"Lizzy!"

Tears streamed down my face faster than I could wipe them away.

"I'm serious, John. I've tried to be strong. I've tried to be patient. And I'm trying to hold out hope that this stupid test will give us an answer and make this all go away. But I'm physically exhausted, my emotions are drained and I feel like shit." Even I had to smile just a little at the unintended pun.

As John looked at me I began to cry even harder than before.

"Seriously, if the rest of my life is going to consist of lying on the couch watching Oprah, while intermittently shitting my brains out then I don't want to do it. This is not who I am!"

My husband sat next to me and held me. While he quietly stroked my hair I cried and cried until there wasn't one more tear left for that day.

◆　　◆　　◆

By the next day I was more composed but still couldn't find anything to eat that agreed with me other than Jell-O. I called Dr. Yamamoto's nurse. She introduced me to yet another diet. This one was called the B.R.A.T diet.

"It's especially good for sensitive stomachs," she explained.

B.R.A.T., it turned out, stands for bananas, rice, applesauce, and toast.

"Try eating little bites of these foods throughout the day," the nurse instructed me. "Popsicles are good too. There's nothing to digest and the sugars might help give you a little boost of energy."

Before we hung up the nurse made an appointment for me to get my test results from the doctor.

In the meantime, John needed to decide if he was going to accept Dan Quayle's job offer to work on his campaign. We discussed our options. We both knew that any political campaign, but especially a presidential campaign, would be a hugely time-intensive process.

John had worked on Reagan's 1980 campaign as well as his 1984 re-election campaign. He knew if he took the job he would be working 10-, 14-, maybe even 18-hour days seven days a week. Plus, Quayle's headquarters were in Scottsdale, which meant we would have to move, at least temporarily, to Arizona.

Initially, John thought it would be a perfect opportunity for me to finally attend the Culinary Institute of America, which had a branch in Scottsdale. He even brought an Institute brochure back from his trip for me.

Taking courses at the CIA had always been something I wanted to do. While it sounded tempting, I had to be realistic. I had done some research in the past years and knew that culinary school was intensive and stressful. How could I attend classes for eight hours a day when I hadn't been successfully away from my house for two consecutive hours in months? As much as I hated to admit it, it wasn't a logical option for me at that time. When the call came from the campaign manager I heard John decline their offer. I felt awful.

"You know," I said as I heard him hang up the phone, "I don't have to go with you. I could stay here with the dogs and keep up the house. You could rent a little apartment close to campaign HQ and it would only be for a year and a bit. You don't have to decline this offer because of me."

"I know," he answered matter-of-factly. "And I didn't. Your health was a part of the decision, but only a small part. I want to write. That's the whole reason we moved out here—to write. I've thought about this almost non-stop since I met with these guys. You and I have talked about the pros and cons and in the end I just don't think I have it in me to go through another campaign. It would be exciting, I can't deny that. But it would also be exhausting and time consuming and it would get me right back where I don't want to be, in politics. Two campaigns and one Administration is enough for me. But thanks for offering. I appreciate it."

"It's a great opportunity, John. I just want you to be sure you aren't turning it down because of me. I don't want you to regret this later on."

"I'm not and I won't. I promise. Now stop worrying, it's not good for you."

Tips and Information

- *Finding a* **Gastroenterologist**. *The best way to find any doctor is by word-of-mouth. Ask your family and friends for referrals. Talk to your hairdresser, pharmacist or massage therapist who may have recommendations of their own.*

  Or try, **www.acg.gi.org**—*the* **American College of Gastroenterology** *website provides a physician locator as well as useful patient information.*

  www.gastro.org—*the* **American Gastroenterology Association** *also has a gastroenterologist locator feature for patients looking for doctors in their area.*

- *Here are a few resources to find helpful information about* **Colonoscopy** *and making it through the preparation:*

  www.medicinenet.com

  www.colonoscopy.com

- *Remember, your doctor and his/her nursing staff are there to help you, their patient. If you have questions or concerns before, during, or after your procedure do not hesitate to ask them questions. Your doctor can't help you if he/she doesn't know you have questions, concerns or fears.*

5

Diagnosis

One week after talking to his nurse, John and I were back at Dr. Yamamoto's office for the results of my colonoscopy biopsies.

I felt a little stronger by then, but still weighed in that day at a minuscule 98 pounds. The doctor took note of my declining weight and asked how I was faring with the B.R.A.T. diet his nurse had suggested.

"Pretty well," I told him. "It was much harder to recover from the colonoscopy preparation than I ever imagined. But, I'm slowly adding other easy to digest foods to my diet. So far, rice, pasta, applesauce, toast, grilled cheese sandwiches and yogurt seem to make my stomach the happiest."

I also admitted that all vegetables and any kind of fruit, other than bananas, were too hard on my system.

"I've stopped eating them but I'm concerned about whether I'm getting enough vitamins into my diet without them," I told him.

"I'm surprised you would have tried them at this point," he answered. "Both vegetables and fruits can be hard on any system. Refrain from eating them, at least for now until your gut has had some more time to heal. Regarding vitamins, you could try a children's chewable, like Flintstones."

"Flintstones?" I repeated, surprised.

"Sure. The amount of vitamins is similar to adult dosages, but since you chew the children's vitamin they should be much easier to digest. Try taking one every other day after a meal, and see how you do. If they work out okay for you, you can take them every day if you wish."

I was still surprised at the idea of a children's vitamin, but decided it sounded pretty logical. When I later read the label on the bottle I realized he was right.

"You could also try adding a can of Ensure to your diet each day," he added. "It's another good source of nutrients and vitamins that should also be easy on your stomach. Start with half a can with your breakfast, then if you feel okay after a few hours, drink the rest."

With the imminent questions of my nutrition answered our discussion turned to my test results. Dr. Yamamoto explained that during the colonoscopy my colon appeared normal.

"I remember you telling me that," John agreed.

"And based on that, I had expected the results of your biopsy to come back negative."

"It didn't?" I asked, grabbing John's hand.

"No, it didn't. The biopsy results show that you have microscopic colitis.

"Microscopic colitis," I repeated with a momentary feeling of relief at knowing what was wrong with me. "I've heard of ulcerative colitis from my dad, but I've never heard of microscopic colitis. What is it?"

"It is similar to ulcerative colitis in that it is caused by an inflammation of the lining of the large intestine. But, unlike ulcerative colitis, it can only be seen through a microscope. With ulcerative colitis there are ulcerations in the lining of the colon, which can cause blood in the stool, as well as cramps and diarrhea. You don't have those ulcerations, and therefore, no blood."

"Can this turn into ulcerative colitis?" John asked.

"We're not sure," the doctor replied. "Microscopic colitis is a very new diagnosis, and just like ulcerative colitis and Crohn's disease we really don't yet understand the cause of these diseases, although there may be a genetic link."

"So what do we do about it?" I asked anxious to get on with making it go away. "How do we cure it?"

"Well, as you probably know from your father, there is no cure for Inflammatory Bowel Disease."

I felt panic settle into my gut. This was the first time I'd thought of what I had as a disease.

"There isn't?"

"Not yet."

"My dad hasn't been sick from this in a really long time," I told Dr. Yamamoto and John. "So maybe he's cured. I know that right after my parents got married he was in the hospital because of a really severe flare-up. In fact, I think they even told my Mom that he could die because he was losing so much blood. And I know when I was younger he used to take these little pills a lot, Lomotil, I think they were. But I don't think he's really been sick from it for a long time. So maybe it just goes away as fast as it comes."

Finally I stopped babbling for a few seconds and just stared at the floor trying to process everything that I'd been told. After a minute or two I looked up and asked Dr. Yamamoto the question that had suddenly entered my mind.

"Could I die from this? Is that a chance?"

"Very few people die from this disease," he leaned forward in his chair and patted my hand reassuringly. "While we may not fully understand IBD, we have come a long way since when your father was probably first diagnosed with it."

He continued to explain that people with colitis can have flare-ups that will last for a couple of days, months or even years. The symptoms can also go into remission just as quickly, again, maybe for weeks, months or years. But that's the frustrating part, he had explained. Even the medical professionals don't know what causes a flare-up, or what causes a remission of the symptoms. While there are new anti-inflammatory medications that seem to be working really well for some people, most people don't stay in remission forever.

"The one thing that is different, though, from previous years, is that we will hopefully be able to control your symptoms, at least somewhat, with medication and alterations in your diet."

"You've called it a disease a few times," John said.

"Yes, that's right. Ulcerative colitis, microscopic colitis, and Crohn's disease all make up Inflammatory Bowel Disease or, IBD for short. Crohn's Disease is more severe, affecting all cell levels of the colon, but you don't have that."

I stared at the floor again feeling like I was having a bad dream. I wished I would wake up.

"I know this has been a lot for both of you today."

Hearing Dr. Yamamoto's voice I realized it was not a dream. This was now my nightmare.

"I'll give you some brochures to take home and read and there's an IBD video you can watch before you leave today. I am also going to try giving you a relatively new drug that has seen very positive results in many patients with MC and UC. The drug is called Asacol, and I'd like you to take two tablets three times a day for the next four weeks. Then we'll meet again in a month to evaluate your progress."

"Has it been approved by the FDA?" John asked.

"Yes. Asacol has been on the market for about two years now, fully approved, and it's part of a new family of drugs that has improved many lives of people with IBD. I'll also give you a prescription for Bentyl, which should help with the cramps and gas. You can continue to take the Imodium if you need it, but don't exceed four tablets per day."

As I took the prescription sheets from him, the tears I'd been holding back spilled over my eyelashes and splashed onto the pieces of paper. I tried wiping the tears away but they just kept coming. John held my hand in his, and gave it a little squeeze.

"I'm sorry Elizabeth. I know this wasn't the news you wanted to hear," Dr. Yamamoto said sympathetically. "And while I can't tell you the road ahead will be an easy one, I can tell you that I have many patients who have learned to live productive and fulfilling lives in spite of their IBD."

He turned to leave then stopped.

"Remember, if you have any questions or problems, don't hesitate to call us. We are here to help you. Okay?"

I reached out to shake his hand. I was able to emerge from my gloom long enough to say, "Okay. Thank you for all of your help."

◆　　　◆　　　◆

As soon as John and I returned home, I called my parents to tell them the news.

"I've got colitis."

The tears welled in my eyes again.

"The doctor said that when he was doing the test he thought everything looked okay. But the biopsies he took showed microscopic colitis."

"Microscopic colitis? What's that?" my Mom asked.

I explained the differences between MC and UC, and that MC can only be diagnosed by looking at the biopsy cells under a microscope. As I listened to myself, I realized that the two illnesses really didn't seem all that different from each other.

"Dr. Yamamoto gave me a prescription for a new medication that's been out for a couple of years," I continued, "And I'm going to have to keep watching my diet, and hopefully that will all help."

I knew my parents were on the line, but their brief silence scared me.

"Mom? Dad? You there?"

"We're here," my Dad answered. "Hopefully the medicine he's prescribing will do the trick. I've read about this new generation of drugs and so far they sound promising. And you've already done a good job of figuring out which foods seem to aggravate things, so be sure to keep staying away from those."

Hearing my dad reiterate much of the same advice the doctor had given helped me to feel more confident. Maybe things really would be okay. My dad is a dentist, and while some people don't consider him to be a "real" doctor, he has always kept up on the latest medical news. Ever since I was a little girl I always felt like he could make everything all right.

"You'll be fine," my mom chimed in, trying to make me feel better. "Look at your dad. He's doing well and hasn't missed a day of work in nearly 30 years. I won't call it good news, but at least now we know what has been causing all of your problems. And like your dad said, hopefully the medicine will help and you'll be back to normal in no time."

"Can you guys come to visit?"

I wanted my parents near thinking that somehow that would make things better.

"Maybe we can," my mom answered without hesitation. "We'll have to check your dad's schedule and flights, but maybe we can make it out to see you for your birthday in September. That's only about six weeks away, which would give you some time to recuperate before we got there."

"That sounds good. Fall is beautiful here and you haven't seen our house yet."

◆   ◆   ◆

I slept fitfully the first night after my diagnosis. My subconscious mind kept going over and over and over all that I didn't know or understand about what was happening to my body. The next morning, John found me clad in my pajamas, hair tousled, punching away at my computer keyboard.

He yawned and rubbed the sleep from his eyes.

"What are you up to so early?"

I was searching the Internet for information on colitis. Determined to find out as much as I could about this disease, I'd been at it since 5:00 a.m. I had already found a number of websites, several chat rooms and ample background information on the subject. I was stunned to find out how many people have this disease considering that, other than my dad, I'd never heard of it before.

"Did you know that, according to the Crohn's & Colitis Foundation of America, there are an estimated one million Americans alone who suffer from IBD?" I told John in response to his question. "And there are just as many men as women who are affected? They also say that while the disease can appear at any age, the age at which patients are usually first diagnosed is 24 years old. And, there are significantly more cases in Western Europe and North America than in other parts of the world."

"I truly had no idea," my husband answered good-naturedly. "Are you planning to take a shower, or should I go first?"

I scrolled down the web page I was reading.

"You go ahead, there's a little more I want to read first."

The CCFA information I'd found also explained that colitis is an inflammatory disease of the large intestine, or colon. It causes inflammation and ulceration of the inner lining of the colon and rectum. At this time, the website did not specifically mention microscopic colitis. Years later, in 2006, I found out they now recognize microscopic colitis in the IBD family.

According to the CCFA website, "The most common symptom of IBD is diarrhea, sometimes severe, that may require frequent visits to the toilet—in some cases up to 20 or more visits per day (I already knew that!). Abdominal cramps are often present, the severity of which may be correlated with the degree of diarrhea present. Blood may also appear in the stools. Fever, fatigue, joint pain and loss of appetite may accompany these symptoms, with consequent weight loss."

According to the Foundation's information, the best-case scenario for colitis patients is that the disease goes into remission and stays in remission. The worst-case scenario is that diet changes and medication stop working altogether and the surgical removal of the entire colon becomes a last resort option. The good news for colitis patients who opt for surgical removal of the colon is that they are cured. The bad news is that they will now live with an ileostomy or external stoma for the rest of their lives.

I suddenly remembered the older gentleman in Dr. Yamamoto's office on that first day.

"Is that what happened to him?" I wondered.

I now felt even more concerned about my long-term prognosis than I had at 5:00 a.m. when I'd started my research.

I headed off to the shower, hoping I would be able to scrub away the disease and the hopeless feelings that had filled my head again.

◆   ◆   ◆

My new daily regimen included taking one tablespoon of Metamucil each morning, six Asacol tablets daily, one Flintstones chewable vitamin with lunch, and one can of Ensure to supplement my bland, boring and vitamin-lacking diet. I made sure I stayed away from all of the foods that were on my "don't eat" list from my elimination diet.

Even with all of these changes, my energy level remained low while my number of daily bathroom visits remained high. My enthusiasm for life was dwindling along with my energy.

I was so afraid of not being near enough to a bathroom or altogether just losing control of my bowels in public that I had pretty much imprisoned myself at home. Some friends wondered why I didn't just wear an adult diaper and get on with life. The simple answer was I wasn't ready to admit defeat. And to me, that's what the adult diaper meant—the diarrhea would win and I would lose. I wasn't fond of losing.

Instead of researching and writing articles or drumming up new public relations clients, I spent most of my time in Internet chat groups with other colitis sufferers. I found a website called *IBD Sucks* (*You bet it does!* I thought) which had a chat room specifically for people with microscopic colitis. The information I obtained from this site was very helpful to my understanding of the disease. I found suggestions from other MC sufferers regarding what did and did not help ease their symptoms. I also got a better idea of what the rest of my life with colitis could hold. Unfortunately, as is apt to happen, most of the personal stories I found on the site were not positive. My fellow colitis sufferers' left me feeling that I would never be the same again, and not in a good way. I had decided that my quality of life would probably only continue to decline.

On one message board I read the story of one woman whose husband of 20 some years just couldn't take the changes that her colitis had brought into their lives and their marriage. Six months after her diagnosis, he moved out. She was served with divorce papers two months after his departure.

Another chat board member said she hadn't been able to hold down a steady job for the past ten years. She could no longer afford health insurance which also meant she couldn't afford her medications. Her condition was worsening each day.

I thought back to my previous professional life in Washington, D.C. Realizing there was no way I could work or live today the way I had during those years B.C., depressed me even more.

I wondered if I would ever be able to hold down a job again.

There was the occasional story of someone whose colitis was in remission and they explained it as feeling like they "had a new lease on life." But, those stories seemed to be the exception rather than the rule. More often, those who had experienced remission for a few weeks, months or even years, admitted that their symptoms did eventually return—sometimes even worse than before. And none of my fellow sufferers seemed to know what they did to get the disease into remission in the first place.

◆   ◆   ◆

As dramatically as I thought our lives had changed when we moved from Washington, D.C. to California, it was nothing compared to the changes that had taken place in the past months. I no longer felt comfortable socializing with friends. If I could actually leave the security of my house and successfully get together with friends, it was inevitable that the conversation would focus around how I was feeling, how thin I looked, and what I could or couldn't eat. Quite honestly, I was embarrassed that my health problems, which were not a very polite subject to discuss over lunch or dinner, monopolized what little time we did spend with friends.

But, leaving our friends aside, John and I hadn't been out together to see a movie or have dinner together in months. The last time we'd tried dinner out, my stomach became so aggravated after the soup that, before our main courses even arrived, we had to leave. John had our meals boxed, and he ate his in front of the television at home while I spent the rest of my evening in and out of the bathroom.

What had been in that soup?! I wondered.

Never had I experienced such a lack of energy as was now ever-present. A big day out for my 5'7", 98-pound body was a trip to the grocery store, or perhaps a walk around the block with the dogs. I was no longer the dynamic public relations executive running from one event or client to another, then partying with friends until the wee hours of the morning. At this point I couldn't even remember what it felt like to have enough energy to keep going from 10:00 a.m. to 9:00 p.m., without a nap, let alone pull an all-nighter.

Very often I didn't get to sleep a whole night through because of the numerous trips to the bathroom. I would get to the point where, after a third nighttime bathroom trip, I would take my pillow and an extra blanket and set up camp on the couch in the family room. It simply made sense. I was close to a bathroom, the television was available to help me pass the long, sleepless hours and John was actually able to get a better night's sleep without me coming and going from our bed throughout the night. But, even though I had figured out a way to deal with my problem and still allow John to rest, I hated these nights. While I was sitting on the toilet or lying on the couch watching infomercials for the George Foreman grill I resented the fact that I wasn't snuggled next to my husband. I wanted to feel his warmth and love surround me like a cuddly blanket.

One of the toughest tolls my colitis took on our relationship in those early years was a lack of intimacy. For me, intercourse was physically painful. Since this had never been a problem before, my gynecologist hypothesized that since I had lost so much weight in such a short period of time, the pain was probably due to the fact that during intercourse, my ovaries were literally being shoved against my body cavity.

But, even if the pain had not been present, I felt anything but sexy or sensual. How could I? I looked like a biology class skeleton, my days and nights were spent pooping, thinking about poop or feeling like poop. I barely had enough energy to sustain myself, let alone make love to my husband. The strain had also taken its toll on my emotional state. I continued to wonder if I would be able to live a "normal" life ever again. And there was a constant flow of questions to which I didn't have answers.

Will I be able to work?

Travel?

Have children?

What will happen if I leave the house?

Will I be able to take care of myself anymore?

Can I trust my body?

Will I ever have sex with my husband again?

With my physical and emotional selves dwindling, I simply retreated to the couch and the bathroom. For six months, I had been robbed of my life as I knew it. I was depressed, and rightfully so.

I had absolutely no idea what the future held for me or for my life with my husband. This disease had affected John's life as well.

I had lost a huge amount of weight in a very short period of time, the medication I was taking didn't seem to be helping too much and John felt at a loss because there seemed to be nothing that he or the doctor could do to stop my seemingly downward spiral.

I would later find out that John's true fear about where my illness could lead came from his sister's death at the early age of 32 from ovarian and intestinal cancers. He remembered that she had also had a sensitive stomach growing up. When she died, the cancer was in both her ovaries and her intestines and the doctors were unable to determine where it had begun. John feared that he might lose me, too.

◆   ◆   ◆

A particularly frightening period of my illness came a year later, in September and October of 1999. I started experiencing episodes of severe lower abdominal cramps. Sometimes the pain and cramping were so unrelenting that I was barely able to sit, stand or speak.

One episode that sticks in my mind started about 10:00 p.m. one evening while we were lounging on the couch watching a movie. The pain that gripped my lower abdomen came out of nowhere and completely debilitated me. When it hit, my body reacted as if I had been shot out of a cannon. I couldn't sit. I had to stand up. But standing up straight made the pain worse. So I bent over at my waist and panted like a dog trying to catch my breath. John had no idea what I was doing and just stared at me with a blank look on his face. As I sank to my knees trying to find any position that was less painful he asked what was wrong.

I could hardly explain it to him. "Terr....i...ble cccraa....mps," I managed to finally get out.

"What can I do for you?" he asked.

By now I had rolled over onto my back, hugging my knees to my chest, "I don't.........kn....ow," I said through the tears that were collecting in my ears.

After suffering like this for ten minutes, John asked if I wanted to go to the emergency room. I really didn't know what to do. But I doubted that I would be able to sit in a car long enough to get there. We decided to place a telephone call to my gastroenterologist first.

John reached the answering service and left an urgent message with them.

Our phone rang a few minutes later. It was one of Dr. Yamamoto's associates.

"My name is Dr. Lieberstein and I'm on call tonight," he told John.

After John explained the situation the doctor instructed me to take two capsules of the anti-cramping medication that Dr. Yamamoto had prescribed for me.

"If the pain doesn't ease in 30 minutes then proceed to the ER," he told John.

Twenty minutes after taking the pills the pain had decreased to a manageable stage and I was able to get upstairs to bed and fall asleep.

The reprieve was short. The pain was back four hours later, but this time it was accompanied by bloody diarrhea.

Up to this point I had never had blood in my stool. I became terribly scared since I no longer had any idea what was going on.

In a panic, I woke John and tried to pull him into my hysterical state. Thankfully, his calm, cool nature prevailed and over the next hours he was able to help calm me down. My husband's continued words of encouragement and hugs made me feel secure.

"Elizabeth, you need to calm down," he said. "You're shaking and panic is only going to make this worse.

"I know," I cried as he held me tightly, "But I don't understand what's going on. It feels like my body is rejecting itself. My gut has totally let loose, and this blood is freaking me out. What does it mean? Why is this happening?"

"I know you're scared. But the doctor did say blood could be a part of this. So there's no reason to freak out. Getting this upset is just going to make a bad situation worse. Here," he said, laying us both down in our bed, his arms still encircling me, "Just lay here with me, and try to relax. You're shaking so hard, your muscles are going to hurt."

"They already do, but I can't make the shaking stop," I told him, feeling a little better from the warmth of his body along mine.

"Shhhhh. Yes, you can," he said in his quiet, calming voice. "Take a couple of deep breaths with me."

As we lay in each other's arms, my husband began taking deep breaths—in and out, in and out, in and out. Soon I was following along with him, and slowly I felt the convulsions in my body lessen and finally subside. My gut seemed to relax as well. Finally I was able to doze off again.

When I woke up in the morning I still had bloody diarrhea. And John had been right. Every muscle in my body felt as if it had been beaten to a pulp. My legs, hips, even my stomach muscles hurt just sitting up in bed.

Before I had a chance to make a follow-up call to Dr. Yamamoto's office, his nurse called the house.

"We understand you called in last night," she said when I answered the phone. "Did the Bentyl help you?"

"It did for a while," I explained, "Then the cramps came back in the middle of the night along with bloody diarrhea. I've never had that before."

"It's not typical of microscopic colitis, but it can happen. Let me talk to the doctor about it and I'll give you a call back."

She got back to me within the hour.

"I talked to Dr. Yamamoto and he would like you to increase the amount of Asacol you're taking to nine tablets per day. Take three at breakfast, three at lunch, and three before bedtime," she instructed. "He is also going to call in a prescription for you for Tylenol 3."

"Tylenol 3?" I asked.

"Yes. It has codeine in it. Some patients in your current situation find that while it helps them to relax a little, it mostly helps to constipate them which should give your colon a break, and a chance to heal a bit."

Desperate, I told her I'd try it. But, I also told her I was a little concerned about taking a narcotic.

"You'll be fine. Just take it according to the doctor's instructions."

An hour later John returned from the pharmacy with my newest prescription for Tylenol with codeine.

"The pharmacy staff asked how you are."

"That's nice," I told him. "I couldn't figure out if it was a good or bad thing that the pharmacy staff knew me by face and name."

Within a couple of hours of taking the first Tylenol I felt better. I wasn't perfect, but my GI tract slowed down enough that I was able to get out of the bathroom for longer intervals which allowed me to get some rest.

The doctor had also increased my dose of Asacol, and over the next week my stomach calmed down measurably. I was spending half as much time in the bathroom as just a week before, and with my calmer gut I actually felt hungry for the first time in months.

I was tempted to eat everything and anything that I hadn't eaten in the past months—apples, potato chips, peanut butter. Common sense prevailed however and I stuck to grilled cheese sandwiches, yogurt, my B.R.A.T. diet, and coconut macaroons.

A friend had sent me an article about a woman with colitis who found that eating coconut helped to calm her gut. It didn't sound anymore far fetched to me than any of the other changes I had made in my diet up to that point so we added coconut macaroons to our pantry. I didn't know for a fact that they were helping, but they weren't aggravating anything and they tasted good. With my most recent crisis under control, I realized that I was on a very slippery slope. Living from one colitis flare-up to another didn't seem to be a good way to live. With a clearer mind and a little perspective I decided that I had to figure out how to take control of my life with colitis as part of it, rather than letting the colitis take control of me.

It's a good idea, I decided. Now I just had to figure out how to do it.

Tips and Information

- *Approximately one million Americans have Inflammatory Bowel Disease.*

- *As many as four million people worldwide suffer from IBD.*

- *An estimated $1 billion in missed work days a year are due to illness from IBD and IBS.*

- *Inflammatory Bowel Disease (IBD) consists of Ulcerative Colitis, Microscopic Colitis and Crohn's disease.*

- *IBD and Colitis websites:*

www.ccfa.org—Crohn's & Colitis Foundation of America (CCFA).
Become a member of this organization today. Your annual dues goes toward research to find a cure for IBD. You will also receive information from the national CCFA chapter and your local chapter which will include information on meetings, events, and support groups in your area.

www.ibdsucks.com—*"Web support for folks with Crohn's, Ulcerative Colitis, Irritable Bowel Syndrome and the like." This site has information and chat rooms galore about every aspect of IBD and IBS. It is an excellent resource for IBD and IBS patients.*

www.ibscrohns.about.com

6

Facing My Fears

During the time I had been experimenting with the elimination diet I had also been seeing a psychologist. In the back of my mind I wondered if stress could be causing my problems. Since my insurance would pay for 50% of the cost, I decided it couldn't hurt.

Dr. Catherine Aisner was the type of woman I could have easily befriended had it not been for our doctor-patient relationship. I was intrigued by her from the moment I found out that she and her husband had a horse ranch in the Carson Valley of Nevada. She was an avid horsewoman who competed in dressage, something I was only vaguely familiar with from stories John had told me about his sister's dressage competitions when she was a young girl. I love animals and had always had a passing interest in horses and riding. This connection helped me to feel comfortable working with a person who had such a passion for her animals.

After my diagnosis and subsequent declining health, I had stopped attending my sessions with Dr. Aisner. I felt the sessions were pointless. I just couldn't understand how talking about my illness was going to make me any better when even the medication I was taking was only now beginning to have an effect.

But, by the time September rolled around I found myself feeling little or no emotion. I had completely taken to the couch, spending my days flipping through the channels on the TV. I didn't care what I watched, or if I watched anything. And to top it all off, the occasional thought   of   *"If-this-is-the-rest-of-my-life-I-don't-want-to-do-it-any-more,"* still ran through my mind.

As each new day dawned, my husband would muster his chipper demeanor and ask me what kind of plans I had for my day. Instead of telling him what I was going to do I would inevitably lament what I couldn't do.

"I would like to go down to Placerville to look through the antique shops," I told him one Saturday.

"That sounds like fun."

"It does. But I can't. I wouldn't even be able to make it half an hour down the mountain before I'd have to go to the bathroom again. And there aren't any bathrooms between here and there. But you can go if you want."

I left him standing in our bedroom looking dumbfounded and feeling at a loss as to how to help me any further.

As if by coincidence, Dr. Aisner called around this time to check in and see how I was faring. I told her about my diagnosis. She suggested we get together later that week to discuss my feelings about it.

"Honestly, I don't know if I could make it through an hour-long session before my stomach lets loose," I told her.

"Well, there's a bathroom right here in the office, you know that, and if you need to take a break it's not going to be a problem."

I was silent as she waited for my answer.

"Let's try it, Elizabeth. I'll put you down for our usual time of two o'clock on Thursday."

For some reason, I didn't argue with her.

When Thursday came I was a little amazed. I had only had three bathroom calls the entire morning and my gut was relatively calm in comparison to previous days and weeks. I was ready to go to my appointment, even a little excited by the outing.

I kissed John good-bye and headed out to the car.

As I began backing down the driveway the urge hit. I slammed on the brakes, yanked up on the emergency brake and bolted for the front door, leaving the car door open and the engine running.

"You okay?" John asked as I emerged from the bathroom ten minutes later.

"Thought I was. But I can't even get out of the fucking driveway."

With my hands perched on my hips I paced back and forth in front of the bathroom door wondering what to do.

"Maybe I should call and tell her I'm not going to make it."

"If that's what you think," he answered, leaving the decision in my hands.

I replied as if he had challenged me.

"I want to go. I really do. I just don't think I can."

"Maybe you should take an Imodium and try again."

"Maybe. I don't know."

I headed toward the kitchen to get an Imodium anyway.

Twenty minutes later and nearly fifteen minutes late for my appointment, I was sitting across from Dr. Aisner. She congratulated me on keeping our appointment and reminded me where I could find the bathroom should I need it.

"It's good Dr. Yamamoto was able to help you find the cause of your problems," she began.

"I thought so too, at first. But finding out really hasn't changed my situation too dramatically. There's no cure. The gastroenterologists don't even understand this disease. And I'll just have to live with this for the rest of my life."

I told her about the colonoscopy, the preparation for the test and how much sicker it had made me. I also shared my experience of culling the internet for information about colitis, and how I had found the various message boards and chat rooms with other people's experiences on them.

"Does the knowledge you've gained from your research make you feel any better about it?"

"Not really," I confessed. "I guess it actually makes me feel more desperate not to have this at all. In some respects my symptoms are pretty typical of the disease, but from the majority of the stories I've read from other people with IBD there doesn't seem to be a lot of hope that it will get much better."

She leaned forward in her chair.

"Elizabeth, try not to let yourself get too wrapped up in other people's experiences. You aren't them, and you really have no idea how this will affect you in the long term. It would be time much better spent to focus on yourself and your own symptoms and how you can learn to control them."

"Okay." I wasn't sure I really understood what she meant. But I had already slowed down on my message board and chat room activities. Reading about other people's experiences had just been depressing me more.

"How does John feel about your diagnosis?"

"He's very supportive," I told her. "Obviously, he wishes I didn't have this, but I do think it makes him feel better to know this is something physical rather than something caused by him or our relationship. I think he's just as scared in some ways as I am, though. Our lives have changed dramatically since this all began and neither of us really knows where this is all headed."

When I first started seeing Dr. Aisner, John had come along with me to a few sessions. He had even attended a couple of sessions with her on his own. She taught both of us a few tools we could use as a couple to deal with our frustrations and the stress and strains that my illness was putting on both of us.

One tool she suggested, that we have since found helpful again and again, was to pretend that we had a shoe box on a shelf. When there is something that one of us wants to talk about but the other person isn't prepared to discuss at that time, for whatever reason, we can put the discussion into the shoe box and then set aside a specific time in the following two or three days to discuss it.

Later on, she would also help us both realize that there are always more than two options, or ways of doing things, for virtually every situation.

"Life isn't an either/or proposition," she explained during one of our sessions.

For example, if we were to make plans to take a hike the next day and I found that my stomach wasn't well that day it wasn't simply a matter of canceling our plans. We had options. We could wait an hour or two to see if my stomach calmed down. Or, we could make alternative plans and go for a shorter walk around the block. A third option is that John could go on without me. Or, a fourth option is that I could go and simply see what happens.

As she explained this, it all seemed so simple, but over the years we would fall back on this more-than-one-option method time and again. It would alleviate much of the day-to-day stress I could feel from the circumstances of my disease.

Dr. Aisner then asked how the diagnosis made me feel.

"It terrifies me," I told her plainly. "Previously my biggest fears had been whether John and I were nuts to give up our corporate jobs to move to the mountains and be writers."

We had had a continual fear about whether we would be able to pay our bills each month. We had wondered more than once if we had been hasty moving so far away from all that was familiar and seemingly secure.

"But now, after the colitis diagnosis and finding out more about the disease I just feel afraid. I feel afraid of things I had never even previously considered could be scary."

"Like what?" she asked, prodding me to think more deeply about what I was saying.

"Well, I'm terrified to leave my house. Just coming here was scary. I'm afraid I'll need a bathroom and won't be able to find one in time."

I confided to her an incident that had happened when John was in Arizona meeting with Dan Quayle. I, a grown adult, had had an accident in the grocery store. I simply did not make it to the bathroom in time, and left the store with my jacket tied around my soiled pants. I was so mortified I couldn't go back to the store for nearly a month afterwards.

"It must have been an awful experience for you. But you seem to have handled it quite well. Also, it's important that you worked through that fear and you have gone back to that store. You've proven to yourself that you can have a successful outing."

"Maybe, but it has also made me realize how little control I have over my bowels at times."

"What other fears are you living with at the moment?"

"I'm always afraid that the frustration might become too much, and John will leave."

I hadn't been able to completely get out of my mind the story of the woman whose husband left her after her diagnosis.

"And sometimes I'm afraid to eat because so often it makes me sick. But on the other hand I'm afraid I'm not eating enough and will keep losing weight and get even weaker and sicker."

Dr. Aisner validated the fears I had shared with her. She told me that I had a right to each and every one of my fears. She also pointed out, though, that I had to be careful not to let my fears take control and become my reality.

She gave me some homework for our next session. I was going to have to dive into my fears further and compile a list of my major fears.

"Focus on those fears that you feel are currently paralyzing you," she instructed me. "Bring your list next week and we'll look at it together and try to understand where each fear is coming from."

◆   ◆   ◆

By our next session I had compiled the following list:

Elizabeth's Fear List

FEAR #1—I fear this disease will dictate what I do and don't do throughout the rest of my life.

<u>FEAR #2</u>—I fear this disease will hold not only me, but John, back from doing what we have talked about doing—and sooner or later he will resent me.

<u>FEAR #3</u>—There are times I'm afraid this disease will only get worse rather than better, or it will stay the same as it is today.

<u>FEAR #4</u>—Almost all of the time, I am afraid of doing things outside of my home away from a readily available bathroom.

<u>FEAR #5</u>—I am afraid I will never be my old self again.

After we settled into our respective seats, I proudly handed my list to Dr. Aisner. She didn't even look at it. She handed it right back to me.

"Why don't you read them to me?"

I was stunned. Thinking about and writing down my major fears had been a very hard thing for me to do. It had taken me days to complete my list. But the thought of reading my fears out loud momentarily paralyzed me. The tears that seemed to be ever-present since my diagnosis once again welled in my eyes.

"I don't know why I'm crying."

"Possibly because admitting one's fears is a very difficult thing to do," Dr. Aisner explained. "Voicing your fears means that you are taking possession of, or owning each one. Once you voice them, you can't hide behind them."

"That makes sense."

I wiped away my tears and composed myself.

Believe it or not, preparing to read my FEAR LIST out loud was perhaps the hardest thing I had ever done in my life. But I did it. I sat there holding my list in my trembling hands and read, out loud, the fears I had been holding inside. It wasn't any easier than I had anticipated it to be. But I actually felt relieved to release the feelings that had been swimming around inside my head for so long.

When I finished, I laid my list aside and closed my eyes for a few seconds taking in what had just happened. My fears were now out in the open, hanging in the air between me and my psychologist, forcing me to face them.

"That's great," Dr. Aisner exclaimed. "Do you feel better?"

I felt slightly like a mole exposed to the bright shining sun.

"I think so. I'm not quite sure how I feel about it."

"Well, your next assignment might help you figure it out. By our next session I want you to root around in your mind and figure out where each of your fears is coming from."

She also instructed me to come up with ways that I could deal with each fear. In order to do this, she wanted me to answer two questions about each of my fears.

The first question I would have to ask and answer was, "What would really happen to me if this fear came true?" And the second question was, "Can the fear come true of its own accord, or do I have any control over it?"

◆   ◆   ◆

Instead of watching more home decorating shows, or wallowing in other people's problems on Oprah, I delved into my own problems. For the next week my thoughts were focused on my fears and the answers to Dr. Aisner's questions about them. By the time I was finished, what I realized about my fears and myself was more liberating than I ever imagined it could be.

FEAR #1—I FEAR THIS DISEASE WILL DICTATE WHAT I DO AND DON'T DO THROUGHOUT THE REST OF MY LIFE.

1) If this fear came true the consequence would be that my life could change in ways that I had not previously considered. But I don't know at this point if those changes would be better or worse than what I imagine.

2) Right now I do think this fear could come true of its own accord. But I am trying to realize that even though the colitis has taken over my life at the moment, I'm not paralyzed, I'm

not blind, and I still have the use of my other major faculties. When I was working at Very Special Arts I saw people with terrible disabilities doing fabulous things with their lives. So I must be able to have some control over how much this disease might affect my life in the future.

FEAR #2—*I FEAR THIS DISEASE WILL HOLD NOT ONLY ME, BUT JOHN, BACK FROM doing WHAT WE HAVE TALKED ABOUT DOING—AND SOONER OR LATER HE WILL RESENT ME.*

1) The consequence if this fear came true could be that John might leave me, or he will start doing things without me. As we both know from some of our previous discussions, John's co-dependent tendencies keep him from doing things he wants to do if I can't accompany him. I, on the other hand, might insist that he go skiing, or for a hike, or on a business trip, and then when he does these things, I feel resentful that I can't go along.

2) This fear can only come true if we both allow it to. The control I have over this fear is to try to do the things that we want to do with the realization that we may need to scale them back in size. Or, perhaps I'll only be able to do a smaller portion of them than John. I will also have to learn to allow John to do things on his own without later making him feel badly that I couldn't be included. John and I will have to work together to not let this fear become a reality.

FEAR #3—*THERE ARE TIMES I'M AFRAID THIS DISEASE WILL ONLY GET WORSE RATHER THAN BETTER, OR IT WILL STAY THE SAME AS IT IS TODAY.*

1) The consequence if this fear came true would be that I would have to adapt my thinking and my lifestyle to what I could do in a given day, week or month. I would have to learn to be more adaptable and to listen to my body's limitations.

2) At this point I don't feel that I do have any control over whether my colitis gets better or worse.

FEAR #4—ALMOST ALL OF THE TIME, I AM AFRAID OF DOING THINGS OUTSIDE OF MY HOME AWAY FROM A READILY AVAILABLE BATHROOM.

1) The consequence of this fear coming true has already happened to me when I had an accident at the grocery store. I was mortified, embarrassed and angry at my body for betraying me.

2) It seems that this fear can come true of its own accord. But, since having my experience in the grocery store I've thought about options that might help me feel more secure. The adult diaper is an option, although at this point I can't bring myself to try it. Not yet. I now always carry a change of underwear and a clean pair of pants in the bottom of my purse. I could get a portable camping potty for the car. Or, if it really became urgent, living in the woods could be beneficial. I could always try to find a secluded tree somewhere and do as the coyotes and bears do!

FEAR #5—I AM AFRAID I WILL NEVER BE MY OLD SELF AGAIN.

1) The consequence would be that there would be a new me and I would have to learn to like and accept her.

2) I don't know if this fear can come true on its own or not. But I do know that I have to at least try not to completely lose the person that I was before this disease came into my life. And perhaps there is even a new me that will emerge because of this disease that won't be so bad either.

◆   ◆   ◆

Thinking about, realizing and writing down the fears that had taken over me was a difficult thing to do. I believe, however, that coming face-to-face with my fears and their potential repercussions, was the first step to digging myself out of the dark pit into which I had fallen since colitis became a part of my life.

Tips and Information

- *Do not be afraid to seek the help of a psychologist or psychiatrist. Being diagnosed with a chronic illness or disease can cause much worry and stress at the least, and depression or suicidal thoughts at the worst. Asking for help to make yourself healthy is a sign of strength, not weakness.*

- **http://helping.apa.org**—*the* **American Psychological Association** *website gives information about the field of psychology, as well as the mind/body connection. Their referral service is available toll-free at* **1-800-964-2000**.

- **www.psych.org**—*website for the* **American Psychiatric Association**.

- *Do not let your personal relationships suffer because you feel ill.*

- *You may want to recommend that your spouse, friend, parent—whomever your "caregiver" may be—make time each day solely for themselves. As the patient, realize that your illness can take a toll on your loved ones, just as it takes a toll on you. Your caregiver may want to seek help from a psychologist or psychiatrist as well.*

- *Acknowledge your feelings about your illness—voice them, write them down, talk about them with a friend. Do not bury or ignore your feelings, they will simply resurface again later on.*

7

Into the Energy Vortex

Starting my weekly sessions again with Dr. Aisner helped. I had been forced to face my fears, and in facing them, I had been forced to look at how I could combat them. The most important insight I had made up to this point was that my illness was forcing me to embark on a journey of self-realization. I knew I had a choice and could choose not to participate in the journey. But where would that leave me?

John was also thinking about my future. While he believed in the doctors I was seeing, and their treatments, he still worried about my low weight, my continuing diarrhea and my constant lack of energy.

He contacted a friend he thought might be able to help.

Thom was a longtime friend of John's dating back to his younger years growing up in Spain. Thom was a newer friend to me. We met when John and I first started dating in D.C. Ironically Thom had recently abandoned his Defense Department job in Washington, D.C. to move to the hills of Prescott, Arizona where he had embarked on the task of writing a book about his spiritual journey. During his last few years in D.C. Thom had met an interesting group of people who cultivated his interest in many New Age areas—healing gems, Tarot, astrological readings, and medicine wheels.

During one of his meditations in his Washington, D.C. apartment, his spirit guides suggested that Thom would soon visit an area where he would see a sign from the Archangel, Michael. A few months later during a visit to Prescott—the picturesque Western

town once frequented by the likes of Wyatt Earp and Doc Holli-
day—Thom saw a sign for the St. Michael hotel and tavern just off
Gurley Street. From previous trips, he already knew and liked Prescott, which is situated in the mountains overlooking the historic Mesa
Verde valley. But, seeing the sign for the St. Michael hotel clinched it.
This was where he was supposed to be, he reasoned. A few months
later he packed up his belongings, quit his job and moved to Prescott.
His new home was situated a mere 30 miles from the glorious red
rock city of Sedona, known among the New Age crowd as one of the
earth's most important energy vortexes. It took little time for Thom
to cultivate a new group of New Age friends.

I knew of Thom's New Age interests but didn't really understand
them. But from the first moment we had met each other Thom and I
had hit it off and I had grown to respect him and his beliefs.

John mentioned my new diagnosis to Thom. He suggested I pay
him a visit in Arizona and get together with a particular friend of his
for a Reiki (Ray-key) session or two.

"My friend is in high demand by a number of doctors in Phoenix
and Flagstaff these days," Thom explained to John. "I'll bet she could
help at least to lessen the severity of Elizabeth's symptoms."

John shared Thom's suggestion with me.

"Reiki?" I asked. "What is it? How does it work? How do you
know it won't make everything worse?"

I dismissed the idea as a bunch of New Age mumbo-jumbo.

John's answer to my questions surprised me.

"Well, I've had my own experience with it. And it's kind of a neat
thing."

"You have?! When?"

I thought I knew everything about my husband. When had he
done *this*?

"Back in '95 when I lived in L.A. for that year," he explained. "I'd
taken a break from writing and had been out backpacking for a few
days in the Plumas Eureka area. When I got home there was a message on my answering machine from Thom. He said that during a

meditation group in Sedona one of the participants told him that his friend, John, needed to come have an energy session with her."

It sounded bizarre but I couldn't help being intrigued. "Why?"

"Apparently I had some holes in my ethereal body that needed to be healed."

"*Holes* in your ethereal *what?*"

"Basically, my aura."

"You didn't go?!" I asked incredulously.

"Hold on, hold on," John hushed me. "I was supposed to be getting back to work on my book, but how could I resist an off-the-wall message like that? I had to go just to see what it was all about!"

"So you jumped into your Jeep and drove 500 miles to have the holes in your ethereal body, whatever that really is, fixed?"

"Yep. I called Thom and told him I'd be there by dinner the next evening."

"Only you," I said exasperated, and a little intrigued at the same time. "So…don't keep me in suspense. What happened when you got there?"

"Well, I got to Prescott the next evening around 6:00. Thom and I hung out on Whiskey Row having dinner and a few drinks. And the next morning I met his friend Katie."

"Is that who he wants me to meet?"

"I think so. I didn't actually ask who he had in mind for you."

…*in mind for me?* I felt like an old maid being set-up on a blind date…. *in mind for me,* I thought again.

"Now stop interrupting and let me finish," he said, pulling me back into his off-the-wall story. "I had an energy session with Katie and while I don't really know if she healed any holes, I do know that by the time our session ended I felt relaxed, content, energetic and very creative. I could hardly wait to get home and get back to work on my book. It was a great experience, Lizzy. Different than anything I had experienced before, but neat."

"Hmmm. Did you ask her what she did to you?"

"No. I just let her do what she did."

"You're weird," I told him.

"Maybe. But it didn't hurt and if nothing else it was a great reason to go to Prescott to see Thom for a few days."

Shaking my head I turned and headed upstairs.

"It's beautiful there, I think you'd really like it," I heard him say as I turned the corner and disappeared.

◆   ◆   ◆

By this point in our relationship John knew me well enough to realize that if he left me alone with my thoughts there was a good chance I would come around and concede to try the energy sessions with Thom's friend. In fact, when I got upstairs I flopped onto my back on our bed and lay there thinking about what he'd just told me. I also thought about what my life had been like since the colitis had reared its ugly head more than a year before.

I was dubious about it all but my curiosity kept tugging at me. I finally decided to call Thom myself.

"I know it sounds weird, Elizabeth," Thom told me. "And I don't really fully understand how it all works. But I've mentioned you to Katie already and she said you are more than welcome to give her a call."

I was silent, considering if I wanted to do that.

"She's done distance healing in the past," he added hopefully, "Even if it only helps you get a little of your energy back, it might be worth a try."

Hearing the concern and sincerity in his voice, I conceded and agreed to get in contact with Katie.

I still had very little idea what Reiki, or energy healing were, but I decided to give Katie a try. Little did I know at the time that throughout the next months I would learn enough about this centuries-old healing method that I would actually receive my own Reiki training and the ability to help heal myself. Without realizing it at this time, I was about to embark on the second stage of my self-realization journey.

◆   ◆   ◆

Later that week Katie and I connected via telephone. She had a nice, calming voice that I immediately liked. I listened to her attentively as she explained how all living organisms are made up of cells, water and energy.

"Sometimes when our body's energy gets out of alignment," she explained, "it can cause illness and dis-ease."

She explained that she could make a better connection with a person's energy if she met with them in person. Not seeing a trip to Prescott, or anywhere else, in my near future, I asked if she could help me long distance as Thom had suggested.

"I can certainly try," she replied. "Send me a photograph of yourself, and I'll see if I can connect to your energy that way."

It still sounded weird and I wasn't sure exactly what I was dealing with. None the less, I popped a photo of myself into the mail the next day and waited for the good energy to come whooshing through the front door and heal me.

Instead, I landed in the hospital a month later with what was diagnosed as my third case of viral meningitis in six years. I was a medical anomaly to the doctors because a person getting meningitis once was weird enough at that time, but three times was virtually unheard of. I was immediately admitted to the hospital. I was confined to an isolation room and hooked up to an I.V. drip antibiotic for the three days it would take the lab to culture my spinal fluid.

"The isolation and antibiotic are just in case it turns out to be bacterial meningitis instead of viral," the doctor told me.

While I understood the reason behind the antibiotics, my gut didn't appreciate them. By day two of the I.V. drip I was, again, experiencing constant diarrhea.

That same day, John received a phone call at our home from Thom.

"Is Elizabeth all right?" he asked. "Katie has had a feeling the last two days in her meditations that she is quite ill. Is it her stomach?"

When John came to visit me in the hospital that day he told me about Thom's phone call.

Since I was possibly contagious John, and all other visitors to my room, were required to dress in a surgical gown, mask, gloves, and booties in order to visit me. I couldn't see John's entire face, but I knew from his eyes that he was serious about the content of Thom's phone call.

After his visit I lay in my hospital bed thinking about John's ethereal body, the weirdness of Katie picking up my current illness in her meditation, and the fact that Thom truly believed in what his friend was saying and doing.

Maybe I was losing my mind. Maybe I was desperate. Or maybe, it just made some kind of strange sense.

"What do you have to lose?" I finally asked myself out loud. "You're at an all-time low in your health, you're probably losing even more weight thanks to the antibiotics, and maybe the energy work will actually help."

By the next morning the results on my spinal fluid were back.

"It's viral, not bacterial," the doctor told me.

I was released from the hospital that afternoon with strict instructions to rest and take it easy for the next few weeks.

As John drove us home I told him I had decided we should go to Arizona to meet Katie and learn more about her energy healing.

"Who knows?" I said, "Either Katie won't be able to help me a bit, or it could be the beginning of something great. No matter what, I'll finally get to see Prescott."

He glanced at me with a sly smile on his lips.

"I guess I'm just desperate enough to try anything," I responded.

◆　　◆　　◆

My decision to go meet Katie proved to be the easy part of the trip. Getting from Tahoe to Arizona proved to be an experience, in and of, itself. This road trip was the first time since the colitis came into my life that I would be shut up in a car for more than the hour and a half trips John and I had occasionally made to Reno.

We decided against flying because of the expense. Between the colitis and my recent hospital stay, my medical bills were stacking up. And, since I wasn't working, and making this trip would take John away from his work for a week, we decided we needed to go the least expensive route we could find. That route was by car.

I mulled the trip over in my mind. Twelve to thirteen hours of driving on primarily desert roads, no cities, and therefore, no bathrooms for hours at a stretch, and a gut that could let loose with nothing more than a moment's notice. This could prove to be my biggest challenge yet.

As we packed our suitcases I pulled three boxes of Imodium out of a Rite-Aid shopping bag. I put two boxes into my suitcase and set the other box aside to be put into my purse.

"There are stores between here and Prescott," John volunteered.

"I know, but if I need it I need it, there isn't always time to go out and buy it."

"Good point. I hadn't considered it that way."

Next, I packed an extra pair of underpants for each day we would be gone and three extra pair of pants.

"Just for piece of mind," I reasoned to myself.

Then, I went down to the kitchen where I gathered together five plastic grocery bags.

"What are you doing?" John asked, "We're leaving the dogs home. We don't need poop bags."

"The dogs won't," I barked at him as I walked toward the stairs. "But I might."

I didn't know exactly what I intended to do with those plastic bags but I had planned to take every precaution possible, and for some reason just knowing the plastic bags would be in the car with me made me feel a little bit better.

I had even researched buying a portable potty from a camping catalogue. It was a good idea for camping in the woods. But I couldn't quite figure out how I would use it on a road trip. Would I set it up along the side of the road and squat for all to see? Or maybe we would make some sort of curtain that John could hold around me. Actually using it inside of our Jeep didn't seem feasible because of space constraints.

For the moment, the idea of the portable potty was ditched.

◆   ◆   ◆

The first morning of our trip we were both up by 7:00. An hour later we were dressed and I was out of the bathroom. John had our luggage packed into the back of the Jeep with snacks and water arranged in a cooler that he fit behind the driver's seat. The dogs were cordoned off in the kitchen for the day and the dog-sitter was set to come feed and walk them twice a day while we were gone. We were ready to begin our Arizona adventure.

John decided to drive the first leg. I belted myself into the front passenger seat.

"Ready to hit the road?" he asked as he started the engine.

My stomach gave a jump underneath the seatbelt. "I think so."

"You don't sound so sure about that."

"Maybe not quite yet," I said as I extracted myself from the car and headed back to the front door.

We made three false starts that morning. Finally, at 10:15 a.m. I was filled up with Imodium and, I hoped, ready to go.

"Can I drive the first leg?" I asked. "Maybe if I put my mind on something else we'll actually get out of the driveway."

"Sure."

We walked around the front of the car to switch seats. As we met half way, John took my hand in his and gave it a squeeze.

"This will be okay. So we're starting a little later than we planned. It's not a big deal. We aren't on any time schedule. Just try to enjoy the journey."

"I will," I told him as he kissed my forehead. "I will."

◆   ◆   ◆

The first few hours of our trip went smoothly. The Imodium-dam in my intestines held and I was able to pass by bathroom stop after bathroom stop. I had even felt hungry enough to pull over at a rest area and have a bite of lunch.

But, a couple of hours later, on the most deserted stretch of road I had ever seen in my life, I actually had to put a suggestion I had read about in an IBD chat room to work for me.

"In a real pinch," the suggestion had read, "When the call of nature strikes and there is no bathroom in sight, park your car as far off the road as possible and away from other cars. Open both the front and back passenger side doors of the car and use them like a bathroom stall while you do your business."

Gross! I'd thought when I read it. *I would NEVER do that!*

We were at least 40 miles from the next town and I simply wouldn't make it. If I had learned anything about my gut with colitis it was that when I felt the urge to go, I had to go, THEN! There was no waiting. No holding it. I was going to have to put the suggestion to work.

While the suggestion proved useful, one improvement I would add for my fellow colitis sufferers is that it is best if the other passenger or passengers in the car get out and take a brief walk while you and nature commune.

John understood my situation and went off to look for arrowheads while I did my business. Five minutes later we were back on the road.

Kingman, Arizona proved to be my next challenge. My gut had been calm since my roadside foray three hours earlier. I had let my guard down enough to lightly doze in the passenger seat.

"We're a few miles from Kingman," I heard John say as Strunz & Farah played in the background. "It should only be another hour, hour and a half after that to Prescott."

"Mmmm, that's good" I purred in my light hazy sleep as music from the CD-bound guitar players swirled through the car.

A few minutes later I jolted out of my slumber. My gut felt like it was being attacked by a knife. My eyes flew open, I bolted upright in my seat and the stabbing pain shot through my gut.

"You have to pull over right now!" I yelled at John.

He jerked the steering wheel to the right and drove through a dirt parking lot slamming on the brakes in front of the dirtiest bathroom door I had ever seen. Graffiti, dirt, wadded-up toilet paper and God-knows-what covered the door's outer surface. By this point in my disease I'd seen the good, the bad and the ugly of public bathrooms. But this was disgusting!

I didn't care. I kicked the door open, ran inside, and dropped my pants. I didn't even realize the toilet wouldn't flush.

A few minutes later John knocked on the door. I didn't answer.

A second later he came in. "I know you don't feel well, but trust me, we have to get you out of here and we have to do it now!"

"I can't," I said from my seat on the toilet. "I think I'm going to need to hunker down here for a bit while I take another Imodium and let it get to work."

"I know that's what you think, and normally I wouldn't argue with you, but I'm asking you to trust me on this one. We need to get out of here and we need to do it now!" With that said, my usually polite and gentle natured husband wadded up some toilet paper, handed it to me and demanded that I get off the toilet.

When I had barely finished buttoning my jeans he grabbed my arm, plunked me into my seat in the car, slammed the passenger door and ran around to the driver's side. He started the engine, threw the car into gear and drove like a bat-out-of-hell until we'd put five miles between us and the Kingman city line.

As he drove, John explained that while I was in the bathroom he remembered either reading or hearing somewhere that Kingman was the cross-roads of a really negative energy vortex.

This was just all too weird. Good energy, bad energy. What was he talking about? What had happened to the relatively normal man I thought I knew? John had always been an avid reader and he was a font of information on nearly every subject known to man. But it was only in these past few months that his knowledge of, and experience with, New Age things had become apparent to me.

Fifteen minutes down the road from Kingman I stopped wondering if he was nuts and wondered if I was. I was *feeling* better. The stabbing pains, cramps, and urgent need to go to the bathroom had subsided as suddenly as they had come on.

"Was it really leaving Kingman that had made me feel better? Or had the Imodium kicked in quicker than usual?"

Whatever it was, I didn't like it and I made a mental note never to go to, or drive through Kingman, Arizona again.

◆　　　◆　　　◆

The next morning I was supposed to meet Katie. I was nervous not knowing what was going to happen or what I was really in for with the experience.

As he dropped me at the front door of Katie's store John reassured me that there was nothing to be nervous about and that everything would be just fine.

"I'm going to go for a hike in the Granite Dells while you and Katie do your thing. But I'll meet you back here in about an hour," he said as I walked toward the store.

"I think I'd rather go with you," I said, turning back toward him.

He reassured me for the hundredth time that morning. "You'll be fine. Stop worrying it will only upset your stomach more."

I raised my eyebrows in response. He knew my stomach was upset because of the two bathroom stops we'd had to make on our fifteen-minute journey between our hotel and here.

"You're going to love Katie and the energy work. I know you will." With that John gave me a tender kiss, scooted me toward Katie's door and headed in the direction of the beautiful red rock Dells that the area is so famous for.

It was hard not to feel calmer in Granite Winds. As soon as I walked in the door I was greeted with a visual and sensory experience—crystals, healing gems, minerals, statues of Buddha, pictures of Christ, aromatherapy candles and incense (which I usually find too strong, but that morning I found them to be soothing), and gentle chimes mingled with soft meditative music that enveloped the air. I drank in the new sights, sounds and smells.

As my eyes wandered through the store I spotted Katie talking on the phone. I'd never seen a photograph of her, but somehow I knew it was her. She was a beautiful woman, in her mid-40's I guessed. She had long, straight, black hair, olive-toned skin, and beautiful chestnut brown eyes. The mustard yellow blouse and large silver and turquoise necklace she wore framed her beautiful, wise, and gentle looking face. When she finished with her call she came over and wrapped me in a huge hug.

"Elizabeth! It's so good to finally meet you."

I was overwhelmed with feelings. In the few minutes I'd been standing in Granite Winds I felt comfortable and completely trusting of this woman I had only just met. Yes, I had talked with her twice on the telephone, but standing there next to her, she seemed to emit a beautiful, calm feeling of pure love and goodness. I had truly never felt anything like it before.

"Your hair is different than in the photograph you sent me," she commented.

"I guess it is," I said as I ran a hand through my chin length locks.

The new hairstyle was another example of the way colitis had changed me. I usually wore my hair cut very short, but since the diarrhea first hit I found it hard to sit in a salon for an hour-long haircut with my stomach rumbling beneath the haircutter's smock. Sudden movements in order to rush off to the bathroom did not make for a good haircut.

As I looked at her hair again I wondered if Katie was American Indian. I later found out that her background is actually a mixture of Polish, a number of different American Indian lines, as well as a number of Mexican Indian lines.

When we had finished drinking each other in Katie led me to a small table in the back corner of her store. On our way there I spotted a partially open door that I quickly recognized as a bathroom. I had become quite adept at deciphering a closet from a bathroom. Knowing it was close helped me to relax even more.

"When I was ten years old I realized my psychic ability," Katie said as we situated ourselves at the table. It looked out over a small garden and meditation circle made from the beautiful red rocks of Arizona. A white candle flickered on the table. Later I found out that white is the sign of purity and tranquility.

"Then when I was eleven," she continued, "My great, great grandfather, whom I had never met when he was alive, appeared to me in a dream. He explained that every human being has an unlimited supply of 'life force energy' that can be tapped to improve health and enhance our quality of life. Grandfather continues to come to me in my dreams and meditations and he teaches me how to best use my gift to heal myself and others."

This was almost unbelievable. I was about to let Katie do something to my energy, which I still didn't fully understand, that she had learned from her dead great, great grandfather!

Instead of getting up and leaving because it just all seemed too weird, I decided to try to understand her better.

"So, is what your grandfather taught you Reiki?" I asked.

"Yes and no," she answered slowly. "What grandfather taught me *is* energy work which uses the life force energy that exists in every human being, which is what Reiki is. But my energy work is really of my own making in conjunction with what grandfather teaches me. I use my psychic ability to see or sense illness in a person, and I also call upon grandfather and my other spirit guides to help me to identify what each of my clients' bodies need in order to heal."

"Hmmm," I replied, still trying to fully grasp the idea.

Two years ago I was working in corporate America thinking that the West coast was full of granola-crunchy hippy people sitting on hills meditating and eating wheat grass. Today I was sitting in a New Age store in the mountains of Arizona surrounded by crystals and incense and listening to a woman tell me that her dead great, great grandfather had taught her how to heal people with energy.

"Pass the granola and wheat grass," I thought.

"All you have to do," Katie told me, "Is relax."

I tried to relax as much as I knew how. Unfortunately that wasn't much. I halfway wondered if I should close my eyes and do a chant. Instead, I watched as Katie's fingers and hands began to move in front of my body. She rubbed her thumbs along her fingertips as her hands seemed to dance in front of me. I didn't understand what she was doing, but as the hour wore on I felt the muscles in my body relax and my stomach actually seemed to unclench. Meanwhile, Katie talked to me.

"There is a greenish fungus in your gut," she explained as her hands began to grab the air in front of me.

"I'm trying to draw some of it out of your system," she continued pulling. "It seems this is something that you may have inhaled many years ago, perhaps from a dumpster or garbage can in a street or an alley."

"That's weird," I said out loud.

"We are going to infuse a healing patch of aloe vera into your stomach that should help to get rid of the fungus."

I expected her to make a paste or something from aloe that we would apply to the skin over my stomach. Instead, her hands did another dance over my gut.

"Okay," she said. "We'll see how that works today and we'll meet again tomorrow morning."

"That's it? But what about the aloe patch?"

"All done. It's not an actual patch. It's aloe energy that I draw from my spirit guides, as well as from grandfather and your spirit guides."

"My spirit guides?"

"Yes. We all have guides who are there to help us as we need them. Your guides might come to you when you meditate or pray," she explained. "And they can help to teach you how to relax, or how to use your own life force energy to empower your mind, body and spirit. So far, Jesus and St. Frances have come to help you."

As my first session with Katie came to an end, she warned that energy work is very intense on the body's cells, muscles, and organs.

"You might feel energized right now."

"I do!" I expounded, interrupting her with my excitement. "I haven't had this much energy in months."

As we walked toward the front of the store she gently rubbed my back with her hand. "Good. But you're going to need to take it easy for the rest of the day. This euphoric feeling will fade and it will probably be replaced with an intense feeling of fatigue. Don't fight it. When you feel tired, relax or take a nap. This will be your first step in learning to listen to your body and hearing what it needs."

"Listen to my body and hear what it needs. That's a new concept," I thought.

Katie also gave me strict instructions to drink at least a gallon of water throughout the rest of the day.

"The water will help flush your system of any impurities that the energy work may have brought to the surface," she explained.

"You'll also need to go to the store. Buy a small spray bottle, distilled vinegar and salt. You will make a solution of one part salt, one part vinegar and two parts water. Then, when you take your shower or bath tonight, and again tomorrow morning, spritz the solution over your body and then wash it off."

My mother had always warned me that oftentimes what I was thinking in my head was written across my face. This time, I knew she was right. The question I had in my mind must have been showing on my face.

"The salt and vinegar will also cleanse impurities from your body," Katie explained.

"Okay," I said.

It sounded bizarre. But I listened because I actually felt better at that moment than I had in months. I had tons of energy. I hadn't thought about my stomach for an entire hour and I was starving!

"You have a nice ruddy color in your cheeks," John said when he came to pick me up.

I decided then and there to do everything Katie said.

"I don't fully understand exactly what Katie is doing," I told him as we drove toward the grocery store, "But we've driven 700 miles, visited 20-some-odd bathrooms along the way and I feel better right now than I've felt in a year. As of right now I completely surrender myself to Katie."

◆   ◆   ◆

Katie had been right. I breezed through the supermarket gathering my supplies from her list, then headed off to have lunch with John—something we hadn't done together for months and months. By the time we returned to our hotel room that afternoon every inch of my body was infused with a weighted feeling of exhaustion that I had never known before. I could barely hoist my legs onto the bed before falling asleep.

When I woke the sun had set and it was time to think about our evening dinner plans.

"Maybe we should just order something in?" John suggested as I brushed my teeth.

"Mmmm," I replied, rinsing the toothpaste from my mouth. "No, how does an Italian restaurant sound to you? Maybe we could invite Thom to join us."

John stood in the bathroom doorway with a Cheshire cat grin smeared across his face.

"What?" I asked. My old playfulness was coming back. "You heard me."

"I heard you, but did I hear you correctly? Lunch out five hours ago, and now you're suggesting we have dinner out with a friend?"

He was still smiling.

"That's right." I wrapped my arms around his neck. "My stomach feels great and I think it would be a nice way to say thank you to both you and Thom for suggesting I do this."

"Well, if you're really sure, I'll phone him right now."

I gently shoved him out the bathroom door. "Go to it. I'll be in the shower, spritzing myself with vinegar and salt."

◆   ◆   ◆

We had a wonderful dinner with Thom at Genovese's, his favorite Italian restaurant in Prescott's old town. By ten o'clock though I was absolutely exhausted again and we declined his offer of a nightcap at the St. Michael hotel. When we got back to our bed and breakfast I donned my pajamas and virtually fell asleep before my head hit the pillow.

When I woke up I was brimming with energy and ready to start my day. John was dead asleep. I nudged him awake.

"Wake up sleepy head."

He turned over and looked at me through half opened eyes. "Huh? What's up?"

"Come on it's time to get going."

He looked at his watch. "Lizzy, what are you talking about? It's one o'clock in the morning."

"It can't be." I looked at the digital clock on the night stand. 1:05 a.m. I walked over to the window and drew back the curtains. It was pitch black outside.

"That's weird," I said, "I'm wide awake."

"I'm not." John turned over and fell back to sleep.

This was the most energy I'd had in months. I grabbed my book and read for a few hours until I was able to fall asleep again.

◆　　　◆　　　◆

The next two days of energy sessions with Katie were even more intriguing than the first day. Part of Katie's method of healing was to scan my body with her hands, finding areas where the natural flow of energy felt blocked and thus possibly causing my illness or dis-ease, as she called it. Then, she would try to reposition or smooth the energy with the help of her spirit guides and my spirit guides.

"There's something between your seventh and eighth vertebrae," she told me on day two. "It relates back to an old boyfriend you had in college. You loved him, but there were many problems in your relationship and it did not end on a positive note."

"That's probably Norman.

"The unresolved issues of that relationship might be the cause of the bouts of meningitis and headaches you've experienced since then."

I was surprised by her suggestion. I hadn't really thought about Norman in years. He had been my first really serious boyfriend and we had even been secretly engaged for a few months during college. But as my interests and my horizons grew he seemed to be stuck in a rut. I was too young and curious to be stuck with him, so I broke things off my senior year of college. He had contacted me my first year in Washington, D.C. but by then I had already met John and my school-girl interest in Norman had evaporated.

"I'm going to see if I can clear out some of the negative energy from your back."

Katie's fingers moved in front of my body as they had the previous day.

"Is that you?" I asked Katie a minute later.

"What do you mean?"

"My spine feels all tingly and like it just got longer and straighter. Now there's a wonderful warm feeling flooding over my entire back."

Her gentle, meditative voice cooed. "Good. That's exactly what we want."

◆　　◆　　◆

"You have a lot of stress stored throughout your body," Katie told me on our third and last day together.

She had focused in on the many feelings I was carrying within me that did not contribute a positive sense of overall health and well-being.

"And it seems that a lot of your energy is tied up in feelings of fear. Fear of failure, fear of success, fear of your stomach problems, fear of embarrassment."

"That sounds about right."

"It's important in learning to heal, Elizabeth, to rid your thoughts and your soul of fear. Fear is our enemy, as it will only hold us back from exploring our true selves, as well as the world around us."

Katie then focused in on the fact that I have a tendency to be extremely hard on myself—a perfectionist in every sense of the word.

"You demand the best of yourself and those around you at all times," she observed. "There seems to be little or no room for errors or differences in your life."

I knew this was true. How many times had John, a friend, or even an employer refrained from voicing a suggestion or small criticism because they knew I would impose far worse self recrimination than was necessary. Katie sure did seem to understand me.

"I know that about myself. But I never realized it could cause a problem with my health."

"Most of us don't realize that. But you need to realize...we all need to realize that making mistakes are a part of our growth process as individuals. Life is not perfect and mistakes are okay. In fact, they are expected, they make us human."

We were silent together for a moment. I let her words sink into my mind.

"I know this is hard for you to realize because you were born under the Virgo sign," she continued, "but it is actually okay and good for us to make mistakes, to not always be perfect. Imperfection is what leaves us with room in our selves and our lives to experience, to grow and to change. If we were all put on this earth as perfect human beings there would be little, if any purpose at all behind our living."

Katie's words had the cogs in my mind racing. I'd never thought along these lines before.

"You also need to realize that you have to put yourself first in life," Katie continued.

Every thought I was thinking must have raced across my face again.

Katie patted my hand reassuringly. "I know, I know. It sounds selfish, and perhaps it is, but who ever said selfishness was bad? Think about it. If we are to be the best person that we can be for ourselves, and therefore, for our loved ones, we have to put ourselves first and admit that there is no more important thing or person than me. Try to release yourself from the pre-existing expectations and identities that your family, friends and co-workers have all put upon you. As the unique person that each of us is, we are not, and cannot be somebody other than who that person is deep down in our soul, stripped of other people's identifying marks."

She was silent for a moment.

"I won't pretend this is easy. It's hard to do," she finally admitted, "And it is a process. But with practice you will learn to allow your true self to come to the surface and be. And when you meet that person for the first time you won't allow her to be buried again because you will be filled with feelings of strength, happiness and honesty."

"Wow," I said. "That's a tough one. I think I understand what you're saying, and I wish I could do that. But…"

"You can, Elizabeth. You can do it. It will take time and a lot of practice. You may even hurt some people's feelings along the way. But you can do it. We all can, if we just try."

"But where do I even begin? I wouldn't even know how to practice."

"Start by feeling. Truly feel and understand each of your emotions as they arise. Feeling your emotions is where you will draw your power. Right now, for example, the over-riding emotion within you is fear. And that fear is taking control of who you are. If you don't face up to your fears, you will become buried in them. Instead, figure out where the fear is coming from…"

I couldn't help it, I had to interrupt her.

"I can't believe you're saying that. This is exactly what I've been working on with the psychologist I've been seeing back in Tahoe—identifying my fears and understanding where they are coming from."

"That's great! You're already on the track to helping yourself heal. Something else I would really like to see you do to help you come into a better understanding of your emotions and to honor the opportunities your emotions give you is through prayer, meditation and positive thought. You don't have to be religious to pray. Say a prayer to whom ever you believe in and give thanks for the opportunity to have and feel your emotions, and to use them to heal your mind and your body."

"I am Catholic," I told her, "So I have no trouble praying. I don't regularly go to church, but I also don't believe that church is the only place where you can connect with God. In fact, I've probably felt closer to God since we moved to Lake Tahoe than at any other point in my life. It's hard not to when the beauty of the mountains, the animals and nature is all around you."

"That's exactly the idea, Elizabeth. What I'm suggesting is that you learn to *feel* your emotions, not just *have* emotions. Learn to open your eyes to the world around you and experience how it makes you feel. If you feel happy or sad or angry or blue, figure out why you feel that way. Don't simply let your feelings exist without understanding them. Honor your opportunity to understand that feeling and thereby learn to understand yourself and who YOU are."

"Okay, so I can fall back on prayer and learn to realize and understand my emotions. But I've never been able to get the hang of meditating. I've tried a couple of times with John, but I don't think I'm doing it right."

She looked at me with a kind compassion in her eyes.

"But see, that's just what I want you to understand. You *can't* do it wrong. There is no right or wrong way to meditate. Meditation is simply being."

"But John always comes away from his meditations with these realizations, or connections that he's made with his sister or father, who are both dead. And I'm just sitting there trying to clear the extraneous thoughts out of my head."

"That's perfect. That's exactly how you begin. Clearing our minds of the many extraneous thoughts that fill our heads throughout the course of a day is extremely hard. And it also takes practice. The more you practice, the more comfortable you will become with yourself and the 'quieted mind' that meditation brings. And, in time you'll come away with your own meditation experiences. But don't compare yourself with John, or anybody else. You have to learn to meditate your own way, to feel your emotions your own way, and to live your own way. There is not just one way to live that is right for all of us."

I heard what Katie was saying, and I really did want to learn how to meditate and feel and heal myself. But I was still confused how to start.

"At this point in my life I've only tried meditating two or three times, but I simply cannot clear my mind of all my conscious thoughts."

"Don't try so hard. Start out by concentrating on your breathing."

I thought about this.

"Close your eyes," she told me a minute later.

"Now?" I asked, getting scared at the thought of trying to meditate in front of her.

"Yes. There's nothing to be afraid of. Just close your eyes and listen to my voice."

I closed my eyes.

"Now, breathe in through your nose and out through your mouth. Again, in through your nose and out through your mouth. In through your nose, out through your mouth."

I don't know how long she continued. It seemed like an hour, but since my entire time with Katie that day was only a total of two hours, it was probably more in the two-or three-minute time frame.

"Now, slowly open your eyes."

I did.

"How did that feel?"

"Good. Relaxing."

"You just meditated," Katie told me plainly. "It's that simple. Start out doing that for five minutes each day then increase your time as you feel more comfortable. Meditation should be soothing, calming and relaxing. It shouldn't be the cause of more stress."

"Relaxing and calming," I repeated. "That's exactly what I'm after."

"I also think the rhythmic breathing could really help when your gut begins to tense or cramp. Try it next time you have a problem and see if it doesn't help to calm things down."

◆　　　◆　　　◆

My time with Katie had come to an end for this trip. I felt like I was leaving a best friend. I was exhilarated by all the things I had learned about myself in the past three days. And I was most excited about all the new tools I had to help myself heal. Unfortunately, the fear I was supposed to be quelling crept into my head as I gave Katie a last hug before we got back on the road.

Katie laid a beautiful tawny colored suede bundle in my hand. The leather was wrapped with a strong waxed twine that was decorated with a variety of red, yellow, and turquoise colored beads and stones, as well as what looked like small bird feathers.

"You'll be fine," she reassured me, sensing my fear. "I've put together this medicine bundle for you."

"It's beautiful," I was enraptured by her gift.

"The contents of the bundle were told to me by grandfather and your spirit guides during my meditations these past three days. In order to make the bundle your own, sleep with it under your pillow for one week and meditate with it each day. During your meditations, hold the bundle in both of your hands and focus your thoughts on the healing that you want to take place within your body. Remember to ask your spirit guides to help you to understand your feelings and to teach you to fight your fear. Over time, the healing properties from the crystals, herbs, stones and feathers that I've put into your bundle will infuse their healing powers into your mind and your body's natural aura."

There were no words I could come up with to thank her for this most special gift. I simply gave her a hug and thanked her through my tears.

"You are an extraordinarily special woman and I treasure the opportunity I have been given to have met you," I said before I walked out the door of her store.

To this day I do not know exactly what is inside my medicine bundle. I improved my meditation skills while making the bundle my own and I continue to meditate with it today. My bundle goes with me everywhere I go. And I find great solace in having it with me during the times when my gut acts up.

Actually Katie had given me two gifts that day. Earlier that afternoon, Katie said her great, great grandfather had welcomed me to call upon him for help in my meditations.

"This is unusual," she explained. "I can only remember a handful of people who grandfather has made this offer to over the years."

I felt honored. But I was unsure how I would be able to contact him. Throughout the next days, weeks and months as I practiced my meditations and slept, grandfather, instead, found me during my meditations and dreams. Even today, he continues to remind me that my ability to heal is in my own will.

"And don't forget," Katie reminded me, "You can call upon your own spirit guides as well. They are always there should you decide to call on them."

She told me that Saint Sophia was a special guide to me and had been present during our sessions together for the past two days.

"That's interesting," I commented out loud, "my maternal grandmother's name is Sophia."

◆　　◆　　◆

Five days after John and I had set out for our adventure in Arizona, I returned to our Lake Tahoe home a changed person. I didn't fully understand all that I had been taught or encountered, but in a strange, blind-faith way, I felt that I now had some very powerful tools I could use to heal my body as well as my mind. I could now call on something stronger than a couch, a television set or a toilet to help me through my days. As I would continue to learn throughout the days, months and years ahead, I could call upon my own will to help and to heal myself.

Tips and Information

- **Reiki** *(pronounced Ray-key) in Japanese means Universal Life Force Energy, or the energy that lives in all living things.*

- *Books that give a good overview of Reiki and how it helps to heal and reduce stress include:*

  Empowerment through Reiki by Paula Horan

  Reiki, The Healing Touch by William Lee Rand

- *Websites that provide more information about Reiki and Reiki practitioners in your area include:*

  www.reiki.org

  http://reiki7gen.com

- *Websites for information and techniques on meditation include:*

  www.meditationcenter.com

  http://stress.about.com/cs/relaxation

8

Logic vs. Faith

A week had passed since our return from my adventures in Arizona and I had been feeling okay. I was not miraculously healed as I had secretly hoped might happen. And while I had been working on my meditation I didn't know if I was really "getting it."

I had, however, put a different tool that Katie taught me to good use—my rhythmic breathing. One night, a few hours after we'd eaten dinner, I was crippled with abdominal cramps. I later explained them to Dr. Yamamoto as feeling like someone grabbed my intestines, wrung them out, and sliced through them with a knife. When they first gripped my gut I couldn't sit, stand, or breathe the pain was so bad. This was similar to the night a few months before when John had called Dr. Yamamoto's answering service.

John held me up as I hunched over. "Lizzy, you have to try to get control."

Tears spilled from my eyes onto our dog who lay below me.

"I ca, can't," I stammered breathlessly in between the sharp stabs of pain.

"You have to calm down," he said. "You're getting yourself into an hysterical state."

I thought the words over and over in my head. "Calm down, calm down, calm down."

It wasn't working. How could I calm down when I was scared half to death? I didn't understand what was happening, and I didn't know what to do about it. The feelings that had enveloped me in Katie's incense-filled store, as well as the many tools she had taught me escaped me in my time of panic.

I was scared by the severity of the pain and didn't know what to do. "Maybe we should just go to the hospital."

"Whatever you think is best."

John is adept at not giving advice or passing judgment on people's thoughts and ideas. I usually loved this trait. That night I hated his response. I knew if I said it again, he would immediately bundle me up, put me in the car and drive me to the ER. I also knew he really wanted me to try to work this out using my new skills.

Mentally, I forced myself back into Katie's store and imagined what she would tell me to do.

"Fight the fear," I finally told myself, "And breathe. Breathe slowly in through your nose, and exhale slowly through your mouth. In through my nose, out through my mouth. In…Out…In…Out…In…Out…"

With each breath I could actually feel my panic slowly subside. I was amazed.

"In…Out…In…Out…In…Out…In…Out…In…Out…"

After five minutes I was able to sit down. I put my head back against the chair and relaxed a bit. I wiped away the last of my tears, closed my eyes and continued to breathe, In…Out…In…Out…John knelt next to the chair stroking my hair.

Five minutes more and the cramps had dulled, nearly gone.

"You look better," he said, breaking the silence.

I was embarrassed at my loss of control. "Sorry about that."

"About what?" he asked. "There's nothing to be sorry about. You did great."

"Great? I freaked out. I was ready to head off to the ER. That's not so great."

"Well, we're not at the ER, and you're no longer in excruciating pain. I'd say that's pretty great."

◆　　◆　　◆

A few days later I had a follow-up appointment with Dr. Yamamoto in Reno. I took my medicine bundle from Katie in the car with me. While John drove I sat in the passenger seat focusing my gaze on the beautiful mountains and my mind on vanquishing the fear of another car trip. We reached Reno with only one bathroom stop along the way. Only one!

"Well, it looks like you've gained a pound," the nurse said with a happy tone in her voice. She jotted down 99 pounds in my chart.

I sat on the crinkly white paper of the examination table waiting for Dr. Yamamoto and thought. For the first time in months, I had actually gained a pound instead of losing a pound. I'd only had to make one bathroom stop to get here. That definitely seemed like progress to me. And it gave me some confidence that I might actually have a little more control over my disease than I had initially thought.

I relayed my experiences with Katie and the energy work to Dr. Yamamoto. He said he'd heard of Reiki, and while he had no first-hand experience with it, he didn't see how it could hurt.

"Keep taking your Asacol though," he advised me.

"I will," I assured him. "I am feeling better, and while I think the energy work and meditation are definitely helping, I agree that it's best to do all of this in conjunction with each other."

"Be sure to keep me up-to-date on what else you learn and how you feel. If you find this really helps you in the long run, it could be useful for some of my other patients as well."

Before he left the exam room I asked if I could ask him a question.

"It seems like whenever I travel the diarrhea is worse. I can't figure out why. Does that make any sense to you?"

"Do you get tense or nervous when you travel?"

"Almost always," I told him.

"The stress probably aggravates your IBS which can also cause diarrhea."

"IBS?! What do you mean my IBS?"

"You've got Irritable Bowel Syndrome as well as colitis. We talked about that the first time I saw you."

I had forgotten him mentioning it during my first appointment. We had talked about so many different options of what could be causing my problems. When he gave me the colitis diagnosis I guess I disregarded the IBS diagnosis.

"So, what does that mean?"

"Nothing really. You're already doing pretty much everything you should be doing. But you do need to learn how to deal with stress better. It's one of the major triggers of IBS."

◆   ◆   ◆

I left the doctor's office in disbelief. I not only had IBD, but I also had IBS. When I got home I headed back to my computer and logged onto the internet. Thirty minutes later I realized Dr. Yamamoto was right. Everything I was doing for my colitis was pretty much the same thing that you do for IBS.

I was surprised by what I had read about Irritable Bowel Syndrome. Over dinner I shared my findings with John.

"It's amazing. This web site I found said that one in five Americans has IBS. That means that 25 to 55 million people in the United States alone have this problem! They also said that it is only second to the common cold as being the most frequent cause of absenteeism from work and school."

"That is amazing. So what's the difference between IBD and IBS?" John asked.

"Well, while IBD is an incurable disease of the colon, IBS is a combination of signs and symptoms that are triggered by food and stress. It's not a disease though, and IBS does not turn into IBD over time. IBS is diagnosed by its symptoms as well as by ruling out other illnesses and diseases first. It's treated with fiber therapy, stress reduction, rest and exercise."

"You're already doing most of those things. That's good news."

"That's what Dr. Yamamoto told me."

We ate our dinner silently for a few minutes.

"I was pretty upset when he told me about this today. But now that I've read a little more about it I realize I've already been dealing with its symptoms simply by working through my colitis. And I guess adding another acronym to my vocabulary really doesn't make my situation any worse."

◆　　　◆　　　◆

I wasn't cured, as I had hoped might happen two days into my energy sessions with Katie. And now I had IBS as well as IBD. But the good news was that instead of making 20 trips to the bathroom each day, I was down to an average of eight to twelve. And while I stayed on my strict diet, I found that I experienced stomach cramps less often, as well as less severely. I was even sleeping a little longer and better at night which was giving me more energy during my days.

When a bad moment did crop up, while my first reaction was still fear, I found my second reaction was to use the new tools I had learned to help me break through the fear and replace it with self-empowerment. That was the most important breakthrough.

"Fear is the enemy," I would remind myself. "I need to fight the fear, to succeed in my happiness."

This was just one of the many mantras that Katie and my spirit guides had given me to help combat the fear I felt.

Other mantras I now used regularly throughout my days included:

I honor my opportunity to help and heal my well-being.

I am my own power, I am my own source.

I choose to release myself of old identities.

Katie checked in with me the first week I'd been back in Lake Tahoe to make sure I was doing okay and remembering my meditation, mantras and to drink eight glasses of water each day.

"I'll continue to send you remote energy," she told me over the phone, "it might work better now that we've had a chance to meet and make a connection with each other. And if you find there are any times when you are having a particular problem, or need a little extra boost of energy, just let me know. It would be best though, if you could come back for another visit in the next six months. In fact, if you're interested, I'll ask my friend who teaches Reiki in Sedona if she has any classes coming up that you could attend."

"Reiki classes?"

"Yes, they will allow you to do some of this energy work on yourself. I can help you somewhat from a distance, but the energy is so much better and stronger in person. We all have an ability to heal, Elizabeth, you just have to continue to learn how to use it."

"Hmmm. I never realized this could be taught."

"It's been taught for years in Asia, it's just recently that we in the Western hemisphere are learning about it."

"I can learn how to heal myself with energy," I thought. *"But, how? Isn't it something you're born with or without?"*

My interest was piqued.

Throughout the next week I resumed my role of researcher. I sat for hours and hours in front of the computer culling the internet for information on energy healing, Reiki and meditation. When I exhausted the internet's resources I headed to the local bookstore, but I didn't find much outside the general meditation and yoga books that my husband already owned. The bookstore owner suggested I visit the local health food store.

"They have a small selection of books," she explained. "But they are more targeted around natural healing methods. You might find what you are looking for there."

At the health food store I didn't find any books on Reiki or energy healing, but I did find a number of recipe books for gluten-free diets, high-protein diets, low-fiber diets, vegetarian diets, and on and on. I wasn't quite ready for any more special diets. The elimination diet had told me that gluten wasn't a problem, so I knew the gluten-free recipe book wasn't necessary for me. And, I was doing pretty well with the changes I had made thus far in my diet.

However, I did pick up a book called "*Prescription for Nutritional Healing*" by Dr. James Balch and Phyllis Balch. The book gives a good general overview of vitamins and minerals and the role each plays in our overall health, as well as a description of what foods are high in each vitamin or mineral. This was especially interesting to me since my diet was still quite limited, and I was occasionally having problems taking even my Flintstone chewable vitamins on a daily basis without causing some upset to my stomach.

The larger bulk of the book, though, is devoted to the more common conditions and illnesses we find in today's society—cold, flu, diarrhea, headache, melanoma, osteoporosis, ulcerative colitis, shingles, tuberculosis, etc. For each condition the husband and wife team gives an overview of that condition and its symptoms. It then follows with sections that provide helpful nutrients and their dosages, as well as helpful herbs and their dosages for each particular illness. And the "further recommendations" section gives helpful tips of things individuals can do to ease the symptoms of a particular illness. For example, in the colitis section it was suggested that the sufferer take acidophilus. I knew yogurt had acidophilus cultures in it but had no idea I could take it as a supplement. I found the pills in the refrigerator section of the health food store. The authors also suggested that peppermint and licorice both aide in digestion—I had already incorporated peppermint tea into my mornings since eliminating coffee from my diet and I liked licorice, too. They suggested a number of things I already knew, but, somehow, reading them in their book made me feel I was really on the right track. For instance, it said that for acute pain you should drink a large glass of water. I had learned this from a friend, but until I read their explanation I didn't know why it helped.

"The water aids in flushing out particles caught in crevices of the colon, often times relieving pain," Dr. & Mrs. Balch explained. (*Pre-*

scription for Nutritional Healing, Second Edition, Avery Publishing Group, 1997)

They also suggested that colitis sufferers conduct a food sensitivity test. I'd already done my elimination diet and knew where my sensitivities lay. So there was no need to do that again.

Over the years I have found the suggestions in this book to be helpful not only with my colitis, but with other ailments and illnesses as well. However, as with all *natural* substances, ALWAYS check with your doctor or pharmacist before taking any supplements and/or herbs in conjunction with other prescription or over-the-counter medications.

In my search for information about Reiki, in addition to a couple of websites I had found, I found two books on the subject. I immediately sent away for them. When they arrived three days later I poured over their contents until I had devoured both.

I found out that the word Reiki in Japanese means Universal Life Force Energy. The first Japanese who used Reiki claimed that we all have Reiki energy within us, but that we must go through an *attunement* by a Reiki Master in order to turn on the energy.

"Once a person is attuned, they can give themselves self-treatments. This is an effective technique for total relaxation, stress release, and realigning the body's chakras. Reiki amplifies the life force energy in our body which helps create balance in the physical and etheric bodies. Treating oneself also helps to release withheld emotions and energy blocks." (*Empowerment through Reiki*, Paula Horan. Lotus Light Publications, 1990-1998)

The self-treatment is what Katie had been telling me about. That could be useful I thought, especially since she's so far away. Earlier in the week I had done a search to locate a Reiki practitioner in my area who I might be able to see locally. But, at the time, I'd found none.

I decided that when Katie's friend in Sedona was doing her next class I would be there. The meditation and breathing were great and since I'd been able to help myself with them, I imagined what I might be able to accomplish with the ability to use Katie's type of energy healing on myself. My feeling of empowerment was beginning to grow.

◆   ◆   ◆

I now decided to share with family and friends all my new-found information from my research and my experience with Katie. I was a little scared because I believed that many of my family members already thought I was nuts after John and I left our corporate America existence and moved off to live like Grizzly Adams in the woods. I still didn't think they all realized that we were living with flush toilets, grocery stores and university educated doctors just down the street from our home. What would they think of what I was going to tell them now? Energy vortexes. Spirit guides. Reiki. Maybe they would try to have me committed!

With this in mind, I decided I could explain my experiences best in writing. I addressed a letter to my parents, my sisters, brother, grandmothers, aunts, uncles, cousins, and close friends. My letter went into great detail about my energy experiences with Katie in Prescott. I told them I realized they may think me a kook, and the energy healing a bunch of mumbo-jumbo (as I had at first), but I asked them to keep an open mind as they read the letter and to realize that I had been feeling desperate, and scared for my health as I made my decision to travel to Arizona. I detailed the feelings of calm and relaxation I had experienced after just one session with Katie. And I wrote that I felt as if I had just a little more control now than before I met Katie. My frame of mind had improved a bit as well.

"I have been feeling better since returning from Prescott," I wrote, "And I am learning to meditate and understand my feelings. I have begun writing much more (as evidenced by this letter) and I am feeling more in control of my health and my life. If you take only one thing that I have shared with you in this letter," I continued, "I believe you, too, will be better off tomorrow than you are today. I know some of what I have told you might sound incredible and you may not *buy* it all. That's okay. It seems to be working for me and since this is the best I've felt in many months I think I'll continue on my journey."

I ended the letter by welcoming my family and friends to ask me questions, question my sanity, or to chalk-up what I was doing as ridiculous. But I reiterated to them that the overall experience had been more positive than I had expected at the outset and I was determined to stick with it and see where the energy healing might take me.

As I popped each letter into the mailbox at the local post office I wondered and worried a little bit how my family would react. To my delight most of them took the same attitude as Dr. Yamamoto. My parents acknowledged that some of it sounded a bit far-fetched, but agreed that if it was helping me even a little bit, they were all for it. I believe the image of my frail 98 pound, 5 foot 7 inch body was probably still fresh in their minds from their trip out West earlier that year.

◆　　◆　　◆

Even though I felt I was now on a better road to health than I had been in the previous year, I still only weighed 100 pounds. My low weight wasn't just obvious to me and John. Friends truly worried about me. Acquaintances seemed concerned.

In fact, one neighbor confronted John one afternoon while I was out and tried to convince him I was anorexic.

"She has to be," the neighbor told my husband. "She's lost a ton of weight since you guys moved in. Or maybe she's bulimic. Have you noticed her spending a lot of time in the bathroom after she eats? It's a tell-tale sign of bulimia."

Not being the kind of person who divulges another's personal business, John tried to convince the concerned neighbor that he knew for a fact I was neither anorexic nor bulimic without telling her what my real problem was.

When he told me about it later that evening, we both laughed. Yes, I did spend a lot of time in the bathroom after meals, but not for the reason our neighbor thought. Maybe some day I would let her in on my embarrassing secret.

The opportunity came a few weeks later when she invited me over for a girls-only happy hour at her house. Obviously I wasn't drinking, but she didn't know that and I decided it was a beautiful evening to spend on the deck with a few of the neighbor women. When I got there I was led to the back patio where an "intervention" was waiting for me. There were three women there who were determined to make me fess-up to my eating disorder. At first I was upset by the whole concept of a bunch of women who barely knew me thinking they had figured out what was wrong with me.

I handled it matter-of-factly, and with a bit of humor. "I'm not anorexic. Although I do spend a lot of time in the bathroom, I don't have an eating disorder. I have a pooping disorder."

My group of saviors was silenced. They did not know how to respond. I spent the next ten minutes laying my medical history out on the table for them to lap up, suspecting that my story would make it through the neighborhood grapevine before the next evening's cocktail hour. When I finished my story I politely stood up, thanked them for their concern and excused myself.

When I walked out the front door, the women were still sitting at the deck table in absolute silence.

In our current society of Jenny Craig diets, Weight Watchers meal plans and low-fat this, and low-fat that, people around me had a hard time understanding that I was struggling to gain and keep weight on. For my problem there was little or no sympathy, unlike that of the overweight person. I oftentimes heard comments such as, "Oh right, like you've ever had to worry about your weight!" Or, "I'd give any-thing to look like you," virtually every day. My reply of, "You don't want to lose weight the way I lose weight," would be met with side-long looks, or rolled eyes. I didn't see the need to explain my medical problem to every woman who felt threatened by my being thin.

The worst comment that was ever hurled in my direction came from a mid-40ish woman I didn't even know. We were in the same aisle of a local grocery store. As I walked further down the aisle away from her I heard her say to her friend, "People like her disgust me. She's so skinny she thinks she's better than us."

I couldn't believe what I'd heard. I turned back to look at the woman who quickly turned and wheeled her cart in the other direction realizing I had heard what she said. My feelings were so hurt by her comment that I left my hand basket filled with groceries on the ground at the end of the aisle and headed out to my car. I sat in the parking lot for the next five minutes and cried.

"How could she say that?" I later asked John after telling him what had happened. "She has no idea who I am, nor what my circumstances are. Instead of leaving, I should have turned around and told her that she too could be this wonderfully thin and unhealthy. She too could feel like shit every day, because all she did was shit all day."

John rubbed my back as we sat together on the sofa. "Sweetie…"

"No, I'm serious," I told him. "People are just vicious for absolutely no reason. I'm sick of it. From now on whenever anybody makes a comment about my weight I'm going to be completely honest with them. I'll just tell them I'm this thin because I have a disease that makes me poop all the time. And most things that normal people can eat make me violently ill. I've pretty much had to completely change my whole life because of my disease. But they should definitely envy me because I can now fit into a size 2!"

"Well, if it will make you feel better, then I think you should do it," John agreed.

Finally venting all the feelings I'd been toting around inside made me feel great. I had owned and understood my feelings like Katie and Dr. Aisner had both told me to do. While I did, once or twice, give people my brutally honest diatribe, I actually found that my sense of humor about "poop" was what seemed to make people want to understand my situation more than yelling at them.

It was weird. While just thinking about my disease or poop even a month before made me feel sad, depressed, or angry, now I was making "poop jokes" at the drop of a hat. I realized that turning this not-so-easy-to-talk-about subject into a humorous situation allowed me to talk about my disease, while making the people around me feel more comfortable with the subject matter. The fact that I was laughing at myself and my disease helped to knock down the taboos that cause polite society not to talk about our natural bodily functions. The more I got back into socializing with friends and letting them know about my condition, the less alone I felt.

It was good to get back to doing something I truly enjoyed in life, being part of social occasions. The more I informed people, the more they were able to understand why I didn't drink alcohol or soda, or eat certain foods. In fact, I often brought my own food with me and there were none of the side-long glances or murmurs behind my back that I had feared. Instead, people came to understand that there would most likely be times when I would simply have to cancel my plans with them at the last minute, or leave a social function earlier than planned.

A particular friend who spent many summer evenings out on his boat knew that the likelihood of my going for an evening cruise was slim, as there was no privy on board. However, instead of simply passing me by as he extended invitations to other friends, he always included me and even offered to make stops back on shore during the cruise if I should find it necessary. I never did take him up on his offers over the two years he made them, mainly because I didn't want to inconvenience him or his boat mates. But it felt great to be included, and to know that I could talk about my disease and its related problems without being shunned.

I also started working again. The real estate agent who had sold us our house had wanted me to work for her ever since the moving truck had pulled up and off-loaded our belongings. While I had done some public relations work for her the first year we were in Tahoe, I had let all of my work opportunities fall by the wayside since the onset of the diarrhea.

One evening, when she and her husband were over for dinner, Theresa asked if I could help her out again. I hesitated. I *was* doing better, I couldn't deny that, but I still had diarrhea, and wasn't in full control of my bodily functions. The thought of putting myself out into the work world for hours at a time frightened me.

I was in an odd situation. In my previous life, B.C., when a job offer would present itself I always looked critically at the job that was being offered. I questioned if it would challenge me enough, considered the salary and made sure there was room for growth within the company or organization. But, not now. This time my only concern was if I could manage working in an office of at least 25 co-workers, three-quarters of whom were female, with only one ladies' room on the premises.

I voiced my hesitance.

"We've got the office set up at the house," Theresa said hopefully. "You can work from there. You could come over for a few hours a day, maybe three times a week, change your environment a little *and* have three bathrooms completely to yourself."

Three bathrooms! The offer was tempting. I looked at John, hoping he would tell me what to do.

Instead he was his usual self.

"It's up to you, Lizzy. Whatever you want to do. But it might not hurt to try."

As I placed scoops of frozen yogurt into dessert cups I mulled over the idea.

I *was* going a little stir-crazy at home now that I was feeling stronger. Getting out of the house and having contact with another person or two might definitely be good for me. And, it could also be good for John to have me up and out from beneath him for a bit each week. He had truly taken on the role of caregiver since my diagnosis. Even though he never complained, I knew the break from worrying about me every time I used the bathroom would probably be as good for him as it would be for me.

I was scared but I knew I couldn't let my fear hold me back any longer.

I took the bowls of frozen yogurt to the table and when I placed Theresa's in front of her I said, "All right. It sounds like it could be good for all of us. Let's try it."

Tips and Information

- *Irritable Bowel Syndrome (IBS) is a functional disorder of the intestine.*

- *IBS cannot be seen under a microscope, and is generally diagnosed by an absence of symptoms. It is a real, physical disorder.*

- *IBS symptoms affect up to 55 million Americans, 80% of those being women.*

- *IBS is only second to the common cold as being the most frequent cause of absenteeism from work and school.*

- *Stress and emotions can be a catalyst for IBS symptoms but they are not the CAUSE of IBS, and IBS is NOT IN YOUR HEAD.*

- *Helpful websites that provide information about the diagnosis and treatment of Irritable Bowel Syndrome (IBS) include:*

   ibscrohns.about.com

   www.niddk.nih.gov/health/digest/pubs/irrbowel/irrbowel.htm

   IBS Self Help Group—**www.ibsgroup.org**

   Irritable Bowel Syndrome Association—**www.ibsassociation.org**

- ***Prescription for Nutritional Healing*** by Dr. James Balch and Phyllis Balch

- *Don't be afraid to explain your illness to family, friends, or co-workers. You will most likely be surprised by their empathy and understanding. And more likely than not they will already know somebody else who has IBS or IBD.*

9

Back in Action

Starting to work again was both hard and good. It was hard because it was the first time with colitis that I had to try to stay on a schedule. This was no longer the working experience I'd had in my B.C. days in Washington. I worked three or four hours at a time, two or three days a week to start. Theresa was very flexible which made it easier for me to feel successful at my new job. There were days when I would show up half an hour or an hour later than we had planned, but by making a quick phone call to let her know what was happening it was never a problem. My new employer understood my illness and was easy to work for which was good because I highly doubted that my ever-changing schedule would have been tolerated by my previous employers in corporate America.

I even found that when I was having a "bad stomach day"—a day that usually would have rendered me a prisoner in my home—if I could just get from my house to Theresa's home office my gut would inevitably calm down an hour or two later. The responsibility of a job was good. I had made a commitment to Theresa and her business, and my responsible nature didn't allow me to just give in to my gut and leave her hanging. I went to work on days that, had I not had that obligation, I otherwise wouldn't have left my house. My confidence in my body was slowly beginning to build, as was my income.

It felt good to get back to work. It felt even better to contribute an income to our bank account again. My salary was small in comparison to what I had been making in Washington, D.C., but I was grateful for the work, the income and the opportunity that I was being given to prove to myself that I could be a productive part of society again. Even with colitis.

◆   ◆   ◆

Nearly two years had passed since Dr. Yamamoto first voiced the colitis diagnosis to me and John. While my colitis was not cured, I had now fully realized that the disease was a part of my life.

I returned to Arizona and took the Reiki I course with Katie's friend in Sedona. It was a beautiful, calming experience that filled me with even more feelings of empowerment. When we got to the part of the course where the Reiki Master administered the "attunement" to me I actually felt my hands get warm, then hot, showing me that the healing energy within my body had truly been released. That second trip driving from Arizona back to my Lake Tahoe home I felt enabled. I was trained and ready to use my life force energy to heal myself when my gut acted up.

In addition to myself, I also practiced my Reiki energy healing techniques on John, my stepson and any friends who would indulge me. I felt like the Reiki was helping me, but I was never really sure if it helped any of my other *patients*.

My answer to that question came a few months after my Reiki attunement. As we watched a movie one evening John complained about a pain he'd been having in his thumb. Never having been a complainer, I knew that for John to bring it up, his thumb had to really be bothering him.

"Do you want me to try some Reiki on it?"

"No, I don't want to interrupt the movie. We can do it later."

"It's okay. I can do it while we watch the movie."

"You can?"

"Sure. Give me your hand."

While we watched the last thirty minutes of our movie I held John's hand in-between both of my hands. When the Reiki energy is "turned on" and working, it still amazes me at how hot my hands become. Usually, I have chronically cold hands, even in the summer. But when I call upon, and use, my Reiki energy my hands become warm, and sometimes so hot I have to run them under cool water.

"It's weird to feel your hands so warm," John commented.

"I know. But it's neat, because it tells me that the energy is flowing.

After thirty minutes I asked John how his thumb felt."

He removed his hand from mine and flexed his thumb a few times. Then he clenched and unclenched his whole hand.

"Wow! That's the first time in the past two days it hasn't hurt."

I was excited that I'd helped him. "Really?"

"Really. Thanks, Sweetie, that's great."

Since my attunement in Sedona I had used my Reiki on myself nearly every day. While my stomach would usually calm during one of my sessions I was never fully convinced that my Reiki techniques had achieved the result.

Maybe it was simply a function of relaxing for twenty or thirty minutes, I would rationalize to myself.

But, here was my husband telling me that I'd helped his thumb. I knew he wouldn't tell me that if it wasn't true. That wasn't John's style. I was thrilled to know that I really could help and heal. The more I used my Reiki and received positive feedback from myself and others, the more empowered I felt with my body's natural healing energy. While I had received my attunement so I could treat myself, I got the greatest pleasure from it when I could help somebody else.

In addition to practicing my energy work, I continued with my meditation and deep, yoga-style breathing. But most interestingly to me, I was learning to listen to my body, and this also helped me to gain back some of the confidence I had lost in the first year after my diagnosis.

It seems simple to me now, but initially I was amazed at what I could learn by simply listening to my body. As I paid attention and listened, I realized that my gut was the most irritable and unpredictable in the early morning. Hence, if at all possible, I simply learned not to make plans until after 10:00 a.m.

I also realized that my Virgo nature—controlled and organized with everything always neat and tidy and in its right place—was part of my problem. It took a while for me to realize that one of the effects of my colitis on my life was that I really couldn't always be in full control.

With a finite amount of energy, cramps, numerous bathroom calls every day and never quite knowing when any or all of these symptoms would hit meant that my life could change from one moment to another with little or no warning. Therefore, I quickly learned that I needed to become more pliable in my every day life. I slowly learned that plans could be changed or canceled and rescheduled as easily as they could be made without huge repercussions.

On many occasions when I had only a limited amount of energy I would realize that everything on my agenda for that day probably was not going to get done. Or, more precisely, things weren't going to get done to my exacting standards. Simply put, I learned not to take life's mundane tasks quite as seriously as I had previously. I came to realize that life would not come to a screeching halt if my kitchen table and counters weren't spotless, or the towels weren't folded and stacked just so, or my shirts weren't ironed with perfect creases down each sleeve. Realizing these simple things helped to alleviate much of the day-to-day stresses that could weigh on my mind and actually cause my stomach to become more upset.

My home is nice, clean, and well-stocked. If I have only a certain amount of time or energy in a given day and I can either choose to clear away the piles of magazines, mail and books that seem to pile up on the kitchen table and counters, or focus on maintaining a healthy and happy sense of self (this could mean meandering an antique shop or book store with my husband, or spending an afternoon reading, writing or meditating), I often choose the latter. I know there will be days when I am forced to stay nearer to home and a bathroom, and much of the household chores can be accomplished then. If I have the energy, focusing on something like housework on a "bad stomach day" can actually help take my mind off of my less-than-settled gut.

In hindsight, it seems a little silly, but I even had to relearn that John and I could leave our home and make a 20-, 45-, or even 120-mile trip away from home—our car trips to Arizona had proved to me that I could successfully leave the safety of my home. I simply had to recognize that there wasn't a set time frame in which a trip had to be completed for it to be successful and fun. I also realized that in America, at least, making a bathroom stop, or two, or three along the way really was very do-able, and usually was a welcome stop for my fellow passengers as well. It's getting a little better in Europe, but public bathrooms are not quite as readily available in many of Europe's smaller cities. I have found in Europe that locating gas stations and train stations along our way are my best bets for finding a public bathroom.

While I have never had to use them, having a change of underwear and an extra pair of pants in the bottom of my shoulder bag helps my confidence immensely. I can go out and still feel "covered" no matter where we go—a hike, a car trip, out for the evening or even on an airplane trip.

◆   ◆   ◆

Even though I have learned how to live with my disease much better today than in its first year or two, I have also learned my limitations.

The most disappointing decision John and I have had to make since my diagnosis was canceling our much-anticipated three-week rafting trip down the Colorado River with friends.

Don and Theresa had already been down the Colorado River once a few years before we met them. During our first year in Tahoe they showed us slides of their trip and told us what a wonderful adventure it had been for them.

"We're signed up to go again two summers from now. You guys should come along," Don exclaimed over dinner one night. "It's a great experience. It's unlike anything you've ever done before."

Before colitis, John and I had been whitewater rafting a number of times on the American River in Placerville and we had both really enjoyed the experiences. We were both excited by the prospect of the Colorado River adventure and decided to send off for information from the outfitter that was organizing Don & Theresa's trip. It wouldn't take place for another two years, but spots on the river are highly regulated and only a certain amount of trips are allowed each year, so you have to plan well in advance. We were told that if we didn't want the two spots, there were plenty of other people who did.

We researched the outfitter that would lead the group, considered the time commitment it would require from us, and weighed if we had the money to make the expensive, three-week trip.

It was clearly going to be the trip of a lifetime. We sent in our deposit to secure our two spaces.

As the commotion of our lives took over the next year, we had all but forgotten the arrangements we had made for the rafting trip until we received a reminder from the river outfitter that the remainder of our fees would come due in three months. By paying the whole fee, we 100% assured our spots on the river trip, but the fees also became only partially refundable should we have to cancel for any reason. And, the nearer the trip date got the less money would be refunded to us if we canceled.

The other information the outfitter sent with the final bill discussed two extra insurance policies they suggested their guests consider purchasing before their trip began—these included out-of-state health insurance and trip insurance. There was also a section that outlined the costs of emergency evacuation—it explained that once we were on the river, the only way to get off the river if you became hurt or ill was via helicopter.

"We need to read all of this closely and consider our options," John mentioned as he paged through the information.

We both read every word of the information packet. We were still itching to make the trip, but had to assess whether I was physically capable of completing the trip.

"I'm wondering what kind of food we'll be eating and if I can request a special diet," I said. "I know it says they will take special requests for low-salt and low cholesterol diets but I wonder what my options might be. My whacky diet doesn't seem to fall into a specific category."

John suggested I call the outfitter and ask them. We were both too well aware of what could happen when I didn't eat according to my special restrictions.

"I'm also concerned about what I do if my stomach goes insane? For example, I've read through their daily schedules and while there is down time off the river we are scheduled to be back on the river at specific times each day. If our group doesn't stay on schedule we would lose our spot on the river. So, what I'm wondering is, what do I do if my stomach goes insane some morning and I can't get out of the bathroom to get into the dory and on the river? It's not like there's a bathroom on the boat."

John nodded. "I've been wondering the same thing. And I don't know the answer. It's probably something to bring up with them when you call about the meals."

Later that day at work I brought up my concerns with Theresa.

"We'll just make sure that Don, you, John and I, are all on the same boat. If you have to go we'll just have a bucket in the back and you can go."

"Theresa! That's gross! What if it happens while we're going through a class III rapid? I'll get flung out of the boat, bucket and all!" I was joking a bit, but was mostly serious.

"Well..." She was stumped.

I decided I had to go straight to the source. Later that week I placed a call to the outfitter. After I explained my specific diet and its restrictions the woman with whom I spoke said it shouldn't be a problem.

"Even though you're out on the river, your guides prepare gourmet meals for breakfast and dinner, with lunch being more of a snack than a meal. You can bring a certain amount of food yourself. But there is quite a bit of variety in the food, and you can ask that yours be a little less spiced or a sauce left off. A couple of weeks before your trip starts you'll have the opportunity to let your guides know about any dietary restrictions you have. It would probably be great for you if you took the job of helping with food prep."

I liked her answer and launched into my next question. I explained my diagnosis of colitis and explained the problems that I can have from it. I was no longer afraid of explaining my disease to people. With great detail I explained how I can need to be near a bathroom for an hour here, ten minutes there or, all afternoon in some cases.

"I don't know," she responded, less helpfully. "You can't really just hang out. Your group will have to keep its spot on the river so the other rafts and dorys don't get hung up. If you can't move with the group, or should become too dehydrated or sick to move on they would need to airlift you off the river."

That was the answer I had feared.

"Is it expensive?" I asked.

"Depending on where you are and how sick you are the costs can hit $10,000 just to get you off the river. Then there could be doctor or hospital costs as well."

Ten thousand dollars! I hated to admit it, but the more I heard and the more I thought about it with my head and not my heart the more I realized I wasn't destined to make this trip. Not at that point in time anyway. The trip was six months away and while I was much better than I had been even six months before, I could still need to use the bathroom up to eight times on any "average" day. A really bad day could still render me useless, sending me to the bathroom 10, 15, even 20 times in a 24-hour period.

After I hung up with the lady from the outfitter, I relayed her information to John. Nervously, I waited for his response.

"Maybe you'd be fine. You've really got things so much better under control."

He was trying to be hopeful and positive.

"Maybe. But when's the last time I was fine for more than five days in a row, let alone three weeks?"

We both sat silently and thought about the answer to my question.

"It's a lot of money to spend just to lose it if I have to be airlifted off the river. Not to mention the $10,000 that could cost in and of itself. And yeah, there is the extra insurance we could buy but that would only bring the airlift cost down by maybe half. I want to go. I really do. But it just seems too huge a gamble for me to take at this point."

We looked at each other. Neither one of us knew what to say next. I broke our silence again.

"I think you should go," I told John honestly. "You'll be with Don and Theresa, and Lynette and DeWitt are going as well. You'll have a great time. I'll be bummed not to be there, but I'll be even more bummed if you don't go just because I'm choosing not to go."

We watched the sun set until the area of the deck where we sat was plunged into shade.

"But this is something I want to do *with* you, not without you," he said.

"I know, but I just don't think it's feasible for me. And I don't want you to miss a great opportunity just because I can't share it with you."

"Let's think about it a while longer," John suggested. "We still have time. The check isn't due for a while yet. Who knows how your stomach will be in another month? You've come so far. Let's just see how you do in the next couple of weeks then make a decision."

The first week after we'd talked about canceling our trip my gut was great. I worked, I went for short hikes, I lived similarly to how I'd lived the first summer we were in Tahoe just at a lower energy level. But, I felt good.

In the middle of the second week my gut exploded. I tried to figure out why. Had I eaten something I shouldn't? Was I stressed? By this time in my illness, I knew that asking these questions was futile. Very rarely, if ever, could I figure out what triggered a "bad stomach day," as I had taken to calling them. But every time it happened, I asked the same questions and came to the same answer, "I don't know what caused it."

I did Reiki on myself, which helped a bit. Meditation helped me to relax and alleviated some of the panic and most of the fear I almost always felt with a "bad stomach day" and I went back onto my B.R.A.T. diet in order to give my gut a break for a few days. But, even with all of my tools employed, my "bad day" had lasted three days, by the end of which I had lost two pounds, and a ton of energy.

A week before the final payment was due to the outfitter I broached the subject with John again.

"So, how do you think I've done these past few weeks?" I asked him.

"Not bad. Better than some weeks. What do you think?"

"Better than some weeks," I agreed. "But definitely not as good as others either. There are a lot of variables to consider, not the least of which is that I've never been out camping for more than a few nights at a time. Then, add my unpredictable stomach, a hefty price tag and, as much as I want to go, I also have to be logical. Logic and my instincts tell me this is a bad idea for me to do right now. I just have the feeling it'll end up like the St. Barth's trip when I was so sick."

Again, we sat in silence for a minute.

"I still wish you would go," I told John. "It's going to be an awesome trip and there really isn't any reason for you not to go."

"Except for the fact that I would rather go with you."

He reached across the couch and pulled me into his chest. We sat together as we both dealt with our disappointment. I cried while he held me in silence. I wondered how many other adventures I would have to forego in my life because of the limitations my health might impose.

Later that fall we gathered at Don and Theresa's house for Thanksgiving. It was both a wonderful and difficult time for me as we looked at our friends' magnificent photographs of the river trip we had missed that summer.

In the end it was a good thing I hadn't gone. During the time our friends were rafting through the beautiful red rock canyons of the Colorado River I was hit with another string of "bad stomach days" that kept me close to home. It is almost a foregone conclusion that had I gone, I would have indeed had to be airlifted off the river, possibly dehydrated and definitely depleted of energy and a large chunk of change.

◆　　◆　　◆

The Colorado River trip was not the first, nor the last time I would be forced to change or cancel my plans. Thankfully my 33rd birthday celebration was not one of those times.

The most beautiful time in the Sierra Nevada's has to be early fall. And since my birthday comes at the beginning of fall, John had suggested that we make a backpacking trip to Round Lake to celebrate.

My first reaction was hesitation. My second reaction was full agreement. After our first year in Tahoe, I had only had the energy to go out on day hikes here and there. I was anxious to try my hand at backpacking again.

We made our plans, gathered our provisions and two days after Labor Day when all the other hikers and backpackers were back at work, John and I and our two dogs headed off on the trail to our campsite six miles away. My energy was good and I hiked well although perhaps more slowly than on our previous backpacking trips.

As we started our hike I had noticed that the waist belt of my backpack was loose even though I had made it as small as it would allow. I decided it wasn't a problem and headed off onto the trail.

An hour later I realized it was a problem.

"I need something to put in-between me and the waist strap of my pack to take up this extra slack," I told John. "The weight of my pack is resting on my hip bones and they're getting bruised."

John had a puzzled look on his face.

"You've never had that problem before."

"I know. But I guess I've also never weighed 108 pounds before when I've used this pack. I should have thought of getting one of those belts with the extra padding that attaches to the pack's waist belt."

After thinking about our options John suggested we improvise. He rolled up my sweatshirt and had me wrap it around my waist. He made a few adjustments to my pack's shoulder straps then tightened my waist belt as tight as he could get it. He pulled so hard he nearly knocked me over.

With my pack more comfortably adjusted we were soon back on the trail. We arrived at Round Lake a few hours later. There were no other campers anywhere. We had seen a couple of day hikers heading in the opposite direction on the trail, but our hopes of being the sole campers had worked out splendidly. We chose the best campsite overlooking the glass-like, blue mountain waters of beautiful Round Lake. Other than the bees that came to share our dinner, we had an evening of fabulous tranquility.

Later that night I emerged from our tent to go on a bathroom run. I looked toward the lake and was confused and awed by hundreds of shimmering lights scattered across the lake's dark surface. I didn't know what it was.

"John! John! Quick come here!"

He had been in a deep sleep, but upon hearing my urgent call he quickly woke up and emerged from the tent.

"What?! Are you okay?"

"I'm fine. Sorry, didn't mean to scare you. But look." I pointed toward the hundreds of little white lights. "What are they? Fireflies?"

John laughed. "No. It's moonlight."

"Moonlight?" I felt silly.

"Moonlight."

He stood behind me and wrapped me in a hug. "Isn't it beautiful?"

"Mmhmmm. But I still think they look like fireflies."

"Okay. They're fireflies. Or, birthday candles. Happy birthday."

"Oh, yeah. My birthday. I guess it must be by now."

The next morning, my birthday morning, I woke first and climbed the rocks that led to a high valley floor. We had decided that our latrine area would be up there safely away from the lake. After taking care of business, I stopped to look at the lake from my higher vantage point. The fireflies were gone, but the lake was just as beautiful. I found a flat rock and sat down on it to view the breathtaking landscape that lay before me.

"I'm living in a postcard," I said out loud to myself.

And I was. The mountain spring-fed lake that I looked over that morning was crystal clear and as still and flat as glass. The granite mountains that surrounded the lake were dappled with green pine trees and aspen trees just beginning to show a hint of their golden autumn colors. They would be glorious in another couple of weeks. I was thrilled to be sitting there on my rock taking in this beautiful scene. I decided to sing Happy Birthday to myself.

The previous few years had been long and hard. They were years dominated with the realities of my illness. But that first morning of my 33rd year, sitting on my rock, looking at the beauty surrounding me and singing Happy Birthday to myself, my stomach and the problems that it could cause were the furthest things from my mind.

We spent the next two days hiking the trails that snaked around the lake and the Sierra Nevada mountain range. As we picnicked in Meiss Meadow, we watched a mother doe and her three young deer feed along the lake's bank, a mere four feet from the trail where we walked. And we enjoyed the ultimate solitude that I have found only in the far-off places where cars, bikes and other man-made conveyances cannot go. I was on my first adventure in years and enjoying every moment of it.

Tips and Information

- *Do not let your IBD or IBS stop you from doing your favorite things—visit an art museum, accept a party invitation, play tennis or golf, or go shopping or antiquing with a friend.*

- *If you go out and try something and have an embarrassing incident, don't stop trying. You haven't failed until you quit trying and quit living.*

- *Have an* **IBD & IBS Emergency Kit.** *It will make you feel more confident and at ease whether at work, at school, a social function or when traveling long distances in a car or on an airplane.*

  Your Emergency Kit might include:

  —Imodium or Pepto Bismol;

  —A change of underwear and/or a change of pants/skirt;

  —An iPod or Diskman so you can listen to soothing and relaxing music;

  —Soothing herbal peppermint or ginger tea bags;

  —Stomach-friendly snacks like bananas, rice krispy treats, bagels or whatever foods calm your gut best.

- *Listen to your body and understand what it is telling you.*

- *Realize that the best-laid plans will sometimes have to be changed or even canceled at the last minute.*

- *Have fun projects, or interesting books, magazines or movies available in case your plans do change and you have to stay close to home and the bathroom.*

- *Be informed when you travel away from home. Know your limitations. And if you are traveling in a group, discuss your disease and some of the problems it can pose with your fellow travelers. It will probably put you and them at ease.*

10

Realizations

As the days, months, and years since the onset of my symptoms go by I have learned two things vital to the success of my daily existence.

First, I have learned not to live *in* my disease but rather, to live *with* my disease. The first year I was diagnosed I lived *in*, and *became* my disease. During that period I lost the thread of who I was and allowed my colitis to become my entire life. I was simply a person who stayed in my home all of the time whether I was actively having problems, or simply anticipating problems from my disease. In my second and third years I learned that my disease was not my entire reality. I am now a person who has a life outside of my home and the bathroom. I have reengaged in the activities of day-to-day living. I shop, I entertain, I go out with my husband and friends, I play tennis, I hike, I live. I know there will be days when I will have to curtail my activities but no longer do I allow my disease and its symptoms to *be* my entire existence.

The second thing I have learned is the power of words. After my diagnosis it was inevitable that whenever I spoke to my parents, in-laws, family or friends, the first thing they would ask was how I was feeling. It was a natural thing to do because my illness had become a very prevalent part of my life since its onset. While I always appreciated the concern for me and my condition it was inevitable that within an hour or two of discussing the status of my gut it would start to act up and cause problems.

"It's as if talking about it jinxes me," I lamented to John after one of these episodes. "I'd swear my gut is listening and says, 'A-ha, so you think you're having a good day? Well, take this!' And wham-o, I'm back in the bathroom."

"Then don't talk about it," John suggested matter-of-factly. "The next time someone asks how you are doing, simply tell them you're fine, but you find it upsets things if you talk about it too much."

"Isn't that kind of rude?" The wanting-to-please-everybody side of my personality was surfacing.

"I don't think so. You might be surprised by how people react."

I tried it. When I mentioned my theory to both my mother and grandmother a few weeks later they both agreed that the more they discussed their aches and pains the worse those aches and pains seemed to become. And when I told friends and other family members that I found talking about my gut just seemed to make it worse, they would respond that they understood and change the subject.

It was a huge eye-opener for me to realize that even though my disease is a physical problem, my emotions and thoughts really could affect my physical well-being.

"Of course they do," Dr. Yamamoto told me when I broached the subject during one of my follow-up exams with him. "Our gut is the root of our emotions. Even people who have no sort of gastrointestinal illness will get butterflies in their stomach, or an upset stomach, or perhaps even diarrhea when they get upset or scared or emotional."

John also noticed that he could tell when I was going to have a problem with my gut a day before the onset.

"You say 'damn' a lot the day before your stomach gets upset," he told me one day in-between my visits to the bathroom.

"*What* are you talking about?!"

"You use the word 'damn' a lot the day before your stomach goes off."

"When did you realize that?"

"I don't know, a few months ago maybe. But even yesterday, you came home, and just in our conversation over dinner you must have used the word 'damn' three or four times."

I was dumbfounded. "Hmmm," I responded. "I wonder if saying 'damn' causes the upset, or is the upset predestined to happen and I start saying 'damn' as a precursor to the upset?"

"I don't know."

Since John's insight I have watched my use of the word "damn." When it slips into my conversation I become very aware of it and try not to use it again. Sometimes my stomach will become upset after saying it and then stopping and sometimes my stomach is just fine. Either way, it was an interesting perception.

Another weird thing we realized about my gut is that when John and I are going our own ways and we say "good-bye" to each other it is almost inevitable that I will have to use the bathroom within the next five minutes. It has even gotten to the point where if I feel the urge to go, but can't, I'll leave the bathroom, find John and ask him to say "good-bye" to me and within five minutes I'll be able to go. It sounds weird, and we agree that it is. But it's just another one of the idiosyncrasies that I have learned about myself from listening to my body. Part of living *with* colitis means listening to your body and paying attention to what you hear—even if it doesn't always make sense, or you don't fully understand it.

◆　　　◆　　　◆

Diet. Meditation. Rhythmic breathing. Reiki. Relaxation. Yoga.

As I incorporated these tools into my daily routine, along with Metamucil and Asacol, I began to regain my health and energy. I spent less time in the bathroom and more time with my husband, stepson, friends and co-workers. I gained back some of the 20 pounds I had lost. By year three of learning to live with colitis my weight was at a constant 110 pounds, sometimes tipping the scales at 115. I was living again. Perhaps not exactly as my life had been before the colitis reared its ugly head, but I *was* living, loving and experiencing life on my own, albeit new terms.

My return to better health was apparent not only to John and me but to my friends, my family, and my co-workers alike. I soon found that people started coming to me with questions they had about certain diets and health problems. When I shopped at Trader Joe's or my local health food store, I would find myself talking with complete strangers about certain wheat-free products I'd tried, the taste of various soy products, or even products I steered clear of that had upset my gut at one time or another. I am always careful not to give, or take too much advice in these situations. I have come to understand that what may work to the benefit of one person, can work to the detriment of another. It all depends upon each individual circumstance. My best piece of advice continues to be that we all have to experiment on our own, with our doctor's advice, and really listen to what our individual bodies tell us is right for us.

For example, while many people with colitis can eat a salad without a problem, I cannot eat even a single leaf of lettuce on a sandwich. If I do, I will experience at least one day of activity on the toilet.

◆   ◆   ◆

By the end of 1999 my gut was calmer and my bathroom calls were less urgent and frequent. I decided to move out of my friend's home office and go to work with her and her husband in their real estate office a couple of miles from my home. The contact I had with other people at the office helped to further build my confidence. Within the next year I decided to study for my California real estate license.

When I first began working with Theresa and Don I knew nothing about real estate. It felt strange to be learning the basics of a new field, when just two years previous I had been at the top of my game in the public relations field. It was a little bit of a slap to my ego, but I was able to get over that quickly simply because I realized I was in a great work situation which easily accommodated my disease.

About six months after I started working for Theresa she offered me the opportunity to become a part of her real estate agent team as well as to continue with my public relations and marketing duties. While I was excelling in the workplace environment, I was unsure about how I could handle my colitis as I spent hours and days showing people homes. The opportunity to make additional money from real estate transactions was a compelling reason for getting my real estate license. But the real impetus was simply to prove to myself that I could do it.

There were certain days where it took all the courage and gumption I had to leave the safety of my home with its private bathrooms and instead spend hour after hour ferrying clients around town from house to house with an unsettled gut that could erupt at any moment. There were days when there was little or no time for Reiki, or when the rhythmic breathing simply did not work and I needed to take two or three Imodium to avoid canceling an appointment with a client.

Just as I had shared the reality of my disease with my family, I had also shared it with my co-workers. But I hadn't made the decision to share certain details of my disease with my clients. After all, these were usually people whom I had only just met. What if I told them about my problem and they then decided to work with another agent?

I wouldn't blame them.

Inevitably, the day arrived when I could no longer avoid the issue. I had an appointment with a middle-aged couple from San Francisco who were looking for a higher-end vacation home. I knew if I could find them the right property it would also mean a nice commission for me.

My clients were driving four hours from the Bay Area to meet with me that day and I had awoken with my stomach on the edge. I had been in and out of the bathroom all morning long. My first instinct was to hole-up at home and take refuge on the couch. I called around to see if any other agents could take my clients, knowing it could also mean losing my commission should they find a house they wanted to purchase that day. It was a beautiful, sunny, warm Saturday and every agent I called was either already out with their clients or out enjoying the weather. No matter how much I wanted to stay within ten steps of a bathroom, I just couldn't bail on my clients.

After our introductions and looking over some information about the properties I intended to show them, we hopped into my car and started off for the first house on the list. By the time we got there I had to use the bathroom.

"This isn't a usual practice," I explained to my clients as I headed to the entry hall powder room. "But it is a bit of an emergency. And I don't think the homeowners should mind."

While I was in the bathroom, my clients showed themselves around the lower level of the house. After we finished looking at the upper level and the backyard, we settled back into my Jeep. Nervously, I decided I had to confide in them in case I had to make another sudden stop.

"Are either of you familiar with the gastrointestinal disease, colitis?"

"I knew somebody once who had it," the wife said. "It was awful."

"It can be. I've got it."

"Oh!" my clients responded at the same time.

"I'm having a little bit of a problem with it today. I should be okay, but there is the chance I may have to make an unplanned stop here or there along our way. Will you be all right with that?"

I was so embarrassed telling these people about my poop woes. I wouldn't have blamed them if they had fled from the car screaming.

"Don't worry about us," the husband replied. "If you need to stop, by all means stop. In fact, it's not a problem if you want to reschedule this for tomorrow. We'll be in town for two more days."

"Thank you, that's very thoughtful. But if you are both okay with it, I think we should continue on. I should be fine. But I did want you to know just in case."

We continued on that day and by the end of our four hours together I only had to make one more bathroom stop. More importantly, I had shared my "secret" with complete strangers and I hadn't been laughed out of the car, shunned or made to feel like I had three heads.

The more clients my boss handed my way, the more people I had to tell about my disease, and with each telling I received 100% understanding. None of them ever minded if we had to linger a few extra minutes at a house or make an extra stop or two at a local convenience store or coffee shop. My clients' acceptance of my situation was a huge relief. It was also another example of facing one of my fears without catastrophic repercussions. I was, indeed, living *with* colitis.

All of the tools that I had learned over the years since my diagnosis definitely helped to improve my health and to make my day-to-day life more "normal." I still had bad hours, bad days and on lessening occasions, bad strings of days. But, I had learned from plenty of experience that when these bad moments surfaced there was no good that would come from panicking, getting angry, scared, frustrated, or even from trying to figure out what-had-set-things-off-this-time.

I had determined over time and many, many hours of trying to figure out why, or what had set my stomach off, that rarely, if ever, would I be able to determine the catalyst for a "bad stomach day."

Instead, I would take the energy that I would otherwise have put into fear or frustration, and would channel it into doing something positive. That could be as simple as realizing that my body needed a break and giving into the "bad stomach day." I could always use the time at home to catch up on my reading, or chat with a family member or friend on the phone with whom I hadn't spoken in a while. It might mean rearranging, or skipping a morning meeting, or beginning my day in the early afternoon after I was able to calm the rumblings in my gut. It could even mean ignoring the rumblings altogether and moving forward with my day as planned. That didn't always work, but I did find on occasion that this tactic would actually help to calm down my gut. And by mid-day I would barely remember the bumpy start to my morning.

When I was a child and didn't feel well, my father used to tell me to get out of bed and get dressed and I would feel better. As an adult there have been many times when I have heeded his suggestion—sometimes it works and I feel better in an hour or two, and sometimes it doesn't and I simply have to give in to a not-so-great-day.

◆   ◆   ◆

One of my new co-workers, Tina, told her boss about her "tummy problems," as she called them, during her job interview. After she was hired, her boss suggested she talk to me since I had stomach problems myself and was doing so much better today than when she had met me a year before.

It turned out that Tina had IBS. She had many of the same symptoms I had experienced and was at a loss for what to do about them. She had seen her family physician but hadn't found his suggestions particularly helpful.

In the first weeks and months that we knew each other we spent countless hours comparing notes on our symptoms, our diets and our lifestyles. I shared my experience with the elimination diet with her. I lent her the many different alternative cookbooks I had accumulated since my diagnosis, hoping that changing her diet might help her as it had me.

The medication Tina's doctor prescribed had helped her somewhat, but it was expensive and her health insurance had stopped covering it. She was just as hungry for information, options and alternative treatments as I had been three years earlier. But most importantly, she yearned to know that she wasn't alone. She read the books I gave her and embarked upon her own elimination diet. Throughout the next months, I was happy to be able to help her during her elimination period with recipes, food suggestions and simple words of encouragement. I was thrilled to know that some of what I had gone through was now helping somebody else.

By the time Tina finished her elimination diet, I was eager to hear her results.

"It's amazing," she told me, "I never would have thought coffee was causing me such a problem, but since I stopped drinking it my mornings are so much better."

She also found, like me, that for some reason yellow corn and products made from yellow corn caused painful bloating and gas. But, for some reason I still don't understand, white corn did not.

I was happy that my experiences were helping somebody else and I was just as happy to realize that I wasn't making some of these things up. I'd wondered if I was nuts at times—able to eat white corn, but not yellow. Who would have thought there was a difference?

It wasn't long before Tina and I became connoisseurs of white corn tortilla chips, as well as soy products. We continued to compare notes. While our illnesses were not exactly the same, the symptoms and even some of the treatments were. It was interesting to find out our similar triggers—things like coffee, corn and oranges that could set my stomach off for a day or more.

It was also interesting and somewhat frustrating to discover those foods one of us could tolerate and the other could not. Tina could drink wine, red or white. For me, just the smell of wine could send my stomach rumbling. As the years passed and my colitis settled into a semi-remission, I have been able to drink a glass of white wine on occasion. But to this day I can't drink red wine.

The most helpful thing for both Tina and me was to find in each other somebody who could understand the frustration, concern, physical feelings and emotional upset that the IBD and IBS caused in each of our lives. While my husband and her fiancée were wholly supportive of each of us, we found an added strength in one another. We could both truly understand each other from actually having been where the other person was. Empathy is nice, but there is no bond like shared experience. I also enjoyed being Tina's mentor. It felt good to take the negatives of my disease and turn them into positives by helping another.

One evening over dinner I mentioned it to John.

"Maybe I'm supposed to take all that I've learned about this disease and dealing with it and help others who are in the same situation I was in three years ago. Maybe this is the positive side to me having colitis."

Another good thing about work was that I met my next Reiki Master. Tina shared her experiences with the elimination diet with one of our co-workers, Irvalene, who told her that she was a big believer in the ability of Reiki to help and heal illness. Tina knew that I had my Reiki I attunement and asked if I knew that Irvalene was a Reiki Master. I didn't. But I was thrilled to find someone else in my own neighborhood who knew and understood the wonderful healing that Reiki can provide. I enjoyed giving myself Reiki treatments, but both Katie and my first Reiki teacher had said that getting treatments from other Reiki practitioners helps to work with energy that I could miss.

Later that year I received my Reiki II attunement from Irvalene. During the classroom work for the Reiki II attunement she explained that it would open my energy fields even further. Now I would be able to treat other people from a distance, as Katie had done for me initially from Arizona, as well as in person. After the attunement I became even more confident in Reiki and in my use of it.

I actually found that giving a Reiki treatment to somebody else filled me with a harmonious feeling. I would come away from giving a treatment to somebody else with a ton of energy and almost always felt better than I had before I gave the treatment. It was a bonus that by giving Reiki treatments to the people that I loved and cared for I was also instilling more healing energy within myself.

When my husband and I moved from Lake Tahoe in the fall of 2002, Tina was scared about whether she would be able to maintain her health without me there to help guide her.

"You'll be fine," I told her. "You know what to do. You've been doing it on your own all along. Just remember to listen to your body and your feelings and use the tools that you now have to heal yourself."

It was almost unbelievable when I heard myself giving her this advice. It hadn't been so long ago that I'd been sitting in Granite Winds in Prescott, Arizona listening to Katie give me virtually the same advice. Now I wasn't just living with colitis, I was helping others learn to live with it, too. Things hadn't come quite full circle but it was a long way from my darkest period.

Tips and Information

- *Know your employment rights by visiting* **The Americans with Disabilities Act** *website* **http://www.usdoj.gov/crt/ada/adahom1.htm**
Or telephone the **ADA Information Line** *at* **1-800-514-0301.**

- *If you are in doubt about possible unfair treatment or discrimination on the job because of your illness, consult a labor relations attorney or the* **Equal Employment Opportunity Commission** *at* **1-800-669-4000.**

- *Realize that there will be some trial-and-error involved in learning which foods agree with your stomach and which foods don't. Once you know your dietary limitations, stick with those foods that work best for you and your stomach. Why risk a relapse by eating the wrong foods?*

- *Keep up with your interests and hobbies.* **Don't** *make IBD or IBS your hobby!*

- *Share your successful experiences of living with IBD or IBS with other patients. We can all learn from each other's experiences.*

- **Natural Health** *is a magazine that provides information on all things organic and natural. This is a good source for information and techniques on meditation, relaxation, yoga, and allergy-free foods and recipes.*

- ***Don't Sweat the Small Stuff...and it's all small stuff*** by Richard Carlson, Ph.D., *is a wonderful* **little** *book that helps to keep life in perspective.*

11

Living

In May of 2000, two years after my diagnosis, John and I decided to try to make our first trip back to St. Barth's. In the past two years we had made short trips within California, to the Midwest to see my family and, of course, the couple of trips to see our friends in Arizona, but we hadn't ventured outside the U.S. since our 1998 trip-from-hell to St. Barth's.

On our short, domestic trips my health had been a mixture of good, okay and outright lousy. There was no getting around the fact that airplane was by far the hardest way for me to travel. Since the onset of my symptoms, air travel had made me nervous. I wasn't nervous about the actual flying part. I was nervous about getting onto an airplane with hundreds of other people and having only one, two, or if really lucky, three bathrooms for all of us to share. I was even more nervous about being held hostage in my seat until the airplane's captain turned off the fasten seat belt sign so that I could move around the cabin and go to the bathroom as necessary.

No matter how much Reiki, meditation or rhythmic breathing I would employ before making a trip via air, inevitably I would wake up the morning I was supposed to travel with a nervous stomach (the IBS part of my illness kicking in). Within an hour of awakening on a travel morning, full-fledged diarrhea would almost always kick in. This didn't just happen on occasion, it happened every single time I traveled via an airplane after the onset of my symptoms back in 1997. Fear was taking over.

Dr. Yamamoto had told me over and over that while stress was not the cause of my colitis, it was a part of my IBS diagnosis.

"Stress is a big part of IBS," Dr. Yamamoto would tell me, "It can and will aggravate your colitis symptoms, causing diarrhea.

Since my normal tools were of little or no help for air travel, I would employ a few other tricks I had learned. I did not like to rely on these second-tier tools for a long period of time, but they can help me to get from point A to point B relatively successfully.

Upon waking on an air travel morning, I would simply let my stomach go for the first thirty minutes and "see what it did." Usually within twenty minutes I would start having one bowel movement after another. By the third bowel movement I would take two Imodium and continue getting ready.

John learned that these particular types of mornings were very stressful for me. He knew I would not be my usual talkative self. In fact, I would keep myself as busy as I could until we had to actually leave the house. I would stop packing and organizing only long enough to eat a cup of yogurt simply so I could take my morning dose of Asacol. If I experienced any more bowel movements I would take another Imodium. As instructed by Dr. Yamamoto when I was first diagnosed, I NEVER exceeded four Imodium in one day, no matter how bad things got. It was a very rare occasion that I ever needed three Imodium to settle things down enough to move forward with my plans.

When it came time to leave the house for the airport, I would do the driving. I found that being the driver, rather than a passive passenger, often helped to take my mind off of my rumbling gut. This way, we would manage to arrive at the airport with only one or two bathroom stops along the way.

My general rule for the rest of a travel day was not to eat anything other than water or Gatorade until we reached our destination. (You can easily take powdered Gatorade in a plastic bag and add it to a glass of water.) The less I put into my body, I reasoned, the less there was to come out of my body. This plan usually worked. If there was any flaw in it, it was simply the fact that by the time I arrived at my destination I was usually hungry and out of energy. I soon learned to pack a plain bagel, rice krispy treats, or a banana in my carry-on bag so that I would have something to nibble on upon arrival at our destination.

It was not the best, or healthiest way to travel, but it usually did allow me to travel successfully from one location to another without the type of problems we had experienced in 1996 and 1997.

◆   ◆   ◆

So, in the spring of 2000 my husband and I successfully traveled to St. Barth's to celebrate our fourth wedding anniversary. By this point in my disease I was pretty well in control of my gut on most days but, there were still times when my gut would simply let loose without warning or provocation. On these occasions there was little time to prepare for the inevitable.

One of our favorite St. Barth's beaches for a quiet, lazy afternoon was Le Petite cul de Sac. Nestled between the lush green hills that comprised the island's landscape, were the calm, clear, bluish-green Caribbean waters of this lagoon frequented mainly by the locals. On our third day John and I swam, snorkeled, sun-bathed, and snuggled with each other all afternoon without another person—or bathroom—in sight.

It had been a wonderful day and we were both happily quiet as we drove back to our bungalow. About half way there it happened, the familiar and unwelcome rumbling in my gut hit.

"We have to find a bathroom," I told John calmly. There was no longer a need for me to become agitated or hysterical. By this time, John had learned that this phrase meant I needed to find the first available bathroom as quickly as possible. He immediately went into detective mode looking for the closest bathroom option.

"Here we go," he said after driving another 200 yards. He pulled into the parking lot of a restaurant where we had had dinner a few nights previously. Before the car came to a complete stop, I had jumped out and headed for the ladies' room. I left John to explain my situation to the staff preparing the dining room for that evening's dinner patrons.

A few minutes later I settled myself back into the candy apple red Moke next to John.

"Why don't we make dinner at the bungalow tonight?" he suggested.

I could feel the paleness of my face overshadowing the sun I'd received that afternoon. I also felt a wave of relief. We had planned to go out to dinner that night and it was wonderful to realize that we had both come to a point where plans could be easily and happily changed to fit my reality without it becoming a huge problem or issue between us.

What a difference this was from our last trip to the island!

◆   ◆   ◆

The success of our trip to St. Barth's buoyed my confidence. I was now ready to embark on one of my biggest tests yet. John and I made plans to spend two weeks traveling with my stepson through Switzerland. After sending Ben back to the U.S. for school, John and I planned to stay another week on our own. It was the first time since my diagnosis that I would spend three weeks on the road. It would also be the first time I would travel with somebody other than John. This trip was the most time John, Ben and I would all spend together outside of my familiar and "safe" surroundings with my disease tagging along.

Over the years I had explained my disease and its complications to Ben. He had seen how it affected my life during his visits to our home at Christmas and the summer. There were many times when he and John would go skiing, or hiking, or backpacking, leaving me behind simply because I either didn't have the energy, a sure enough stomach, or the confidence to go along with them on a particular adventure.

One of the most important coping skills I had learned for dealing with colitis and how it could affect other people in my life was communication. I had never had a problem talking "poop" with John, or my parents or even my good friends. Eventually, I could even talk candidly to my co-workers and real estate clients about my situation. But I found talking about my personal "poop" problem with my stepson a little more daunting. It was a bodily function, after all, that an adult is supposed to have full control over. The topic, quite frankly, was gross. I worried that it would make Ben feel uncomfortable with me.

I couldn't have been further off base.

Even though he was an 18-year-old with a limitless amount of energy, Ben was empathetic. He was concerned about me and how I was feeling even before our plane left Reagan National Airport in Washington, D.C.

This was the trip where my communication skills, being-able-to-change-plans-at-the-last-minute skills, and knowing-when-to-give-up skills were put to the test.

It happened our first week when we were in the Bernese Oberland area of Switzerland. This is the region everybody thinks of when they read the book, *Heidi*. Swiss chalets built of caramel-colored pine line the rolling hills of the lush green land. Window boxes spill over with red, yellow, purple and white flowers. And cows with tinkling bells around their necks can be seen and heard around every twist and turn. On one of our walks, Ben and I were befriended by a white-and-brown calf with large, gentle brown eyes. He probably would have followed us home if the farmer hadn't come out to retrieve him. We were all having a wonderful time.

One evening at dinner John, Ben and I had discussed our activity options for the next day. We decided to go to the top of one of Switzerland's tallest mountains—the Jungfrau. We consulted the train schedule we had picked-up at the Zurich airport and decided to take the 10:00 a.m. train. This meant we would have had to leave our chalet by 9:30 a.m. to have enough time to park, purchase our tickets and board the train. The day we had planned to take the train to the Jungfrau I woke at 8:00 and my stomach let loose five minutes later. My first reaction was panic.

As I sat on the toilet listening to John and Ben begin their preparations for the day, I tried to calm myself.

"Panic is not going to help," I said out loud, "You know that."

I also knew that these episodes could get worse just as easily as they could get better. There was virtually no way for me to tell if this episode would last for a couple of hours or for a couple of days.

I didn't want to risk ruining the day for all of us. I decided to tell John and Ben to go on without me.

When I voiced my opinion to them a few minutes later, thankfully neither of them wanted to leave me behind.

"Well, then what are our options?" I asked.

John pulled out the train schedule. While he and Ben perused it at the kitchen table I headed back to the bathroom.

When I returned to the kitchen Ben had a suggestion.

"It looks like we could get on a 10:45 a.m. train. Would that work?"

I unwrapped a chewable Imodium then gave John one of my knowing looks. I chewed and swallowed the turquoise colored tablet and wondered if I would ever get used to the chalky, fake mint flavor.

John was still looking at the train schedule. "We *could* get a train at 11:30, or 12:15. Either of those would still give us plenty of time to look around at the top, have a little lunch and do the hike down the mountain we discussed last night. What do you think about that?"

I looked at the clock, 9:45 a.m. Nearly an hour and a quarter until we would have to leave in order to get on the 11:30 a.m. train It might be doable.

"Maybe. But I feel badly making you guys hang out while there's still the chance that I won't be able to make it."

John and Ben looked at each other then back at me.

"I think we should see if you can go," Ben said. "You'll feel better. And anyway, you can't miss the Jungfrau!"

With an extra hour and a bit, I decided to get to work. The Jungfrau was waiting. And so were John and Ben. As I headed to the bathroom once again I decided it was time for another Imodium. This was not usually my first choice of defense, other than where airplane travel was concerned.

But, drastic times called for drastic measures, I thought.

After the bathroom, I went off to our bedroom to meditate and do a short Reiki session on myself. John and Ben hunkered down on our chalet's balcony overlooking the Swiss Alps and Lake Thun. Ben had found a pile of National Geographic magazines to look through. John was perusing the guidebook we had brought along with us.

One hour and two bathroom trips later I was nervous but I was also ready to see how things went on the way to the train station.

I found John and Ben reading in our chalet's living room.

"You guys must be pretty bored."

"Out of my mind," Ben replied simply.

I laughed at his honesty. I was bored out of my mind, too, and ready to change my surroundings.

"Well, I appreciate you waiting for me so patiently, I really do."

"You're welcome," they both replied.

"I figure if I can get from here to the train station without a problem I should be okay," I told the guys. "And once we're there, the stations and the trains have bathrooms, so that part of it will be a piece of cake."

Most trains in America have bathrooms. When I saw the train that would take us to the Jungfrau I became worried. It was a beautifully restored, old wooden train with plank seats. It was reminiscent of the trains I used to ride on as a small child at the Milwaukee County Zoo. I walked up and down the track twice looking at each car of the train. There were no bathrooms on board.

I grabbed John away from the ticket kiosk and explained the situation to him.

"What will I do if I have to go?"

"I was just talking with the ticket agent. She said there are two stops along the way. We can always get off, and as long as everybody keeps their ticket stubs we can get back on and continue the journey."

"That's true. The train stations all seem to have bathrooms. Okay. Buy me a ticket," I told him. "I'm on board."

"Oh God!" Ben exclaimed at my bad pun, "You must be feeling better."

I guess I must, I thought. Telling bad jokes was always a good sign.

We only had to get off at one stop. And, it turned out to be a false call—just a little gas that was no big deal. We were on another, more modern, train five minutes later and back on track. Up and up and up we went as the train chugged toward the top of the mountain. Right before we reached the summit, the cloud level encircled us and the Jungfrau disappeared from view. There wouldn't be any panoramic vistas for us that day.

It didn't matter, though. We had all marveled at the beautiful scenery on the way up. When we disembarked the train at Europe's highest railway station I could definitely tell we were at high altitude. As we approached the station the conductor told us we were at an altitude of 11,333 feet. He advised that we walk slowly until our bodies got used to the thinner air.

Because of the clouds and rain enveloping the Jungfrau we were unable to witness the supposedly spectacular 360-degree panoramic view from Europe's highest observation terrace. Instead, we followed Ben to the Ice Palace inside the glacier. It was amazing to walk through a glacier. The freezing cold, blue glacier ice had been carved and sculpted into a maze of paths filled with beautiful ice sculptures and patterns.

After a leisurely lunch it was time to embark on the five-mile hike down the mountain to the valley.

I changed plans on the guys one more time.

"What would you think if I met you guys in Wengen?"

"Why?" Ben asked. "I thought we were going to hike down."

"Well, I want to, but I'm just feeling kind of pooped out from this morning."

"Pooped out? Liz!" He couldn't believe I'd done it again.

"Oops. I didn't do that on purpose," I told him. "Really."

"What are you thinking?" John asked.

"Well, my ticket is still good, so I can take the train back down to Wengen. That's the little town where we stopped on the way up so I could use the bathroom. Remember?"

They both nodded.

"I noticed that the hiking trail you'll be on goes right through the town square. The weather's nice down there and I figure I can hang out for a couple of hours while you guys hike down. Depending on how I feel when you get to Wengen I can either do the rest of the two-mile hike with you, or take the train down the rest of the way."

"You sure?" John asked.

"Mmhmm. I'll be able to chill out in the sun for a bit. Maybe check out a shop or two in the village and then I'll see you when you get there. It's not that I don't want to do it, I do. It's just that I don't think I have enough energy to keep up with you guys the whole way down. I'd rather be able to hike part of the trail, than none of the trail."

With our new plan set, I headed for the next train, leaving John and Ben to meander their way down through the gorgeous towering peaks that are the Swiss Alps.

Had this whole situation taken place a year or two previously, I would have insisted that morning that John and Ben go to the Jungfrau without me. I would have spent the rest of the morning and probably part of the afternoon in and out of the bathroom feeling physically depleted, emotionally sorry for myself and resentful at not sharing in the adventure.

Our day had not played out exactly as we had planned it the previous night. But, with a little Reiki, a little more Imodium and a lot of patience and understanding from all three of us, we had a day filled with beautiful scenery, great experiences and even better memories.

Boy, have I come a long way, I thought that night as I fell asleep with the day's memories turning into my night's dreams.

◆   ◆   ◆

When our stay in the Bernese Oberland came to an end, the three of us drove to the Vallemaggia (major valley) in the section of Switzerland that borders Italy. We spent three days in this beautiful region filled with mountains, rivers, waterfalls and little stone villages. We spent our days walking the many, many trails that wind through its series of valleys. We barely made a dent in its 435 miles of hiking and walking paths.

Our evenings were spent soaking up the Mediterranean flavors of the local restaurants. The entire region was settled by Italians. And as we spoke Italian and ate pasta, braised rabbit and real Neapolitan-style pizza, it was hard for me to believe we were in Switzerland and not Italy.

The few days we spent in the Vallemaggia took me back to 1988 when I had lived with my aunt and uncle in Naples, Italy. My uncle was in the Navy, and they had been stationed in Naples for seven years at that time. I went to visit them after working tirelessly for six months on Herb Kohl's U.S. Senatorial campaign in Milwaukee. I had intended to visit them for two weeks before heading back to Wisconsin to start my junior year of college but ended up staying in Italy for four months instead. I loved my time with my aunt and uncle in Italy. I still look back at the memories of that time fondly. Now, I was a part of Ben's first trip to Europe. This was the type of experience I thought colitis had robbed me of. But, here I was enjoying Europe with my husband and stepson. I was truly *living* with colitis.

Tips and Information

- *When you join the* **Crohn's & Colitis Foundation of America (www.ccfa.org)** *you will receive a membership card. The back of the card reads…* I CAN'T WAIT! Thank you for understanding. The bearer of this card has a medical condition that requires him/her to use bathroom facilities urgently. Thank you for your cooperation.

  I have used this card many times in an emergency and have never been turned away from the front of a line, or private store bathroom.

- *Plan vacations/trips that will be as flexible as you need to be. A group tour to Europe with a strict day-to-day schedule may not be the best idea for someone with IBD or IBS. Instead, plan a self-guided trip or take a cruise that will provide more flexibility in your schedule.*

- *Check into traveler's insurance before you leave home on a trip. Each companies polices will cover different things. Look for policies that include everything from trip cancellation, to trip interruption, to baggage delay, medical expenses, lost or stolen baggage, and rental car collision damage waivers Call your health insurance company before you leave home to verify if you have medical coverage outside your immediate "home" area. Also check what types of coverage you may already have with your AAA membership or credit cards.*

- *If IBD or IBS does disrupt your plans while on vacation, simply have a discussion with your other travelers and decide what activities you can and cannot participate in.*

- *When traveling by airplane, alert your flight attendant about your IBD or IBS before an emergency strikes. Usually they are quite helpful in making a lavatory available to you when you need it.*

- *If traveling to a foreign country, learn a few key phrases in the native language before you land. The words for pharmacy, diarrhea, cramps and stomach are all helpful. Also, learn the phrase for* **"Where is the nearest toilet?"**

- *Make sure to take with you any prescription medications you may need while away on your trip. Take along enough medication for two or three days longer than you plan to be traveling. Pack half of them in your purse or carry-on, and the other half in another piece of luggage. This way, if one piece of your luggage is delayed, lost or stolen you still have some medication readily at hand.*

- *Remember to take along the name and phone number of your doctor and the prescription bottles for your medications.*

12

C'est la vie

In the beginning stages of my disease, when I was at my most depressed, I could see no way back to my old life and being "normal." Even though it's hard for me to admit now, I had even contemplated suicide once or twice. Thankfully I hadn't had the guts to act on those feelings. For as frustrating and debilitating as it can sometimes be, I've come to realize that colitis and its associated symptoms are not worth losing one's life over.

My future seemed bleak and hopeless at the beginning of my illness. Fortunately, I had a patient husband, some great doctors, friends, family and even a few strangers to help me along the way. With a lot of hard work, patience and determination to overcome my illness, I have since realized that what I was experiencing was simply one of life's roadblocks.

IBD and IBS are not fatal. I remind myself of this fact nearly every day. Some days, those of us who have these problems, might wish they were fatal. However, while I have realized that my disease is something that is a continual challenge, I now know that neither IBD nor IBS have full *control* over me.

Had I been given the choice whether to have colitis or not, of course I would have chosen not to have it. However, like so many other people who are learning to live *with* their disease, whatever it may be, I was not given a choice about whether to have, or not to have IBD or IBS. The choice I *was* given, however, was whether I would let either of these take control over my life, or whether I would take control of it.

I am glad that I opted to learn how to take control and worked through my depression, my frustration, my anger and my fear.

While I now better understand how my disease affects my body than I did in 1998, I am still always learning. I continually find out new things about myself, my illness, the steps forward that the medical field is taking to more fully understand and treat IBD and IBS, as well as how to live within the physical limitations that I still experience at any given time on any particular day.

I now have many more symptom-free days than I had in the first few years of living with my disease. I am also now able to maintain a relatively constant weight somewhere between 115 and 118 pounds. But, I also still have "bad stomach days" that can cause my weight to plummet by one, five, even ten pounds in certain instances. Instead of fear now being my first reaction to a "bad stomach day," oftentimes frustration creeps in instead. Frustration at having my life interrupted. Frustration at not being able to identify the trigger or catalyst that caused my colitis to flare up. But I am no longer frustrated or scared at not knowing what to do to help myself relax, heal and continue to live my life.

The many tools that I now possess to help cope with those "bad stomach days" are a strong arsenal. I can put them to work for me any time, anywhere, as long as I remember they exist. I am no longer defenseless against colitis.

My "bad stomach day" tools have helped me to work through "bad stomach days," "bad stomach weeks," and "bad stomach months" and are invaluable to both my physical and emotional well-being.

Instead of my fear list, I now live with my "tool list" which you too may find helpful.

Elizabeth's "Bad Stomach Day" Tools

- Meditate for ten, twenty or thirty minutes to help myself relax.

- Give myself a Reiki treatment.

- Remove as much stress from my life as possible.

- Alter my diet until my gut calms so that it can heal.

- Read a book, listen to music or talk to a friend—anything that will take my mind off of my gut.

- Take an Imodium on those extra bad days when I can't give in.

- Lean on friends and family.

- Simply give up for a day. Know that "giving up" is not a sign of weakness, but rather a sign of strength because I now know when my body needs rest in order to heal.

- Maintain control of my body and my life by realizing that sometimes I will have to change or alter my plans.

- Remember that there is always more than one option for any situation that may come along. Knowing that I have options helps to alleviate stress.

◆　　　◆　　　◆

It may sound odd, but it is true to say that since the onset of my symptoms I have become a stronger person. I have a better understanding of my body and its needs. Plus, John and I have a stronger, more understanding and patient relationship with each other than we did before my diagnosis.

Because of the challenges John and I faced in our marriage as a result of my illness, we have both learned much patience, tolerance and pliability. We have both gained an ability to make changes in our schedules simply because we have to. We have come to realize that change is not the be-all end-all, it is simply a change. We are more patient with each other now than before. And we appreciate each day we are allowed to spend with each other, happy, healthy and strong of mind, body and soul. We embrace life completely and take nothing for granted.

I have also learned that while changing your life or lifestyle can seem difficult, it is really quite easy once you make the commitment to do so. All the things I used to make fun of West Coast granola-crunchies for have now become an integral and important part of my life—alternative foods, Reiki, meditation, yoga, stress reduction, fresh air, drinking eight glasses of water a day, and positive thought.

For the first two years after my diagnosis symptom-free days were few but when they were present I quickly learned to take advantage of them. That could mean anything from taking a walk through our neighborhood or a mountain meadow to visiting with friends, or jumping into the car to drive to the local shopping mall. I realized that every symptom-free day was a gift and was not to be taken for granted.

◆   ◆   ◆

I believe an important thing for you, the reader of this book, to remember is that just as there does not seem to be one set of symptoms that all IBD or IBS sufferers experience, there also is not one set of "tools" that work for all people with IBD or IBS. What I have outlined in this book is what has helped me to get a handle on my disease and to be able to lead a more fulfilling and productive life. If any of my "tools" work for you I am happy to have you adopt them into your own life. Chances are that with your own research, your relationship with your doctor, and some trial and error, you will find additional "tools" that fit your specific situation and life.

My final thought is for you to realize that very few, if any of us, will ever fully understand the *why* of our illness. So, instead of trying to figure out *why* we are ill, or *why* we are having a "bad day," I recommend focusing your attention on finding out *what* helps you to live a healthier, happier and more rewarding life within the limitations that your illness can impose at any particular time. Keep your sense of humor, engage in those hobbies and interests that make you happy and surround yourself with friends and family who prove helpful to you.

Inflammatory Bowel Disease and Irritable Bowel Syndrome are nuisances. But remember, plenty of people live full and complete lives despite their IBD or IBS—Dwight D. Eisenhower, 34th president of the U.S., had Crohn's disease; John F. Kennedy, 35th president of the U.S., had ulcerative colitis; Mary Ann Mobley, actress and former Miss America, has Crohn's disease; actor John York, who plays Mac Scorpio on General Hospital, has ulcerative colitis; and, president George W. Bush's brother, Marvin Bush, has ulcerative colitis.

You, too, can live successfully despite your disease—just remember to take it one day and one step at a time.

Tips and Information

- *Make the most of the new you. Share your successes with other IBD or IBS patients. It will help buoy their spirits and prove that we can live despite our illness.*

  Share via internet chat rooms like **www.ibdsucks.com**. *Or, in the support group sections on the Crohn's & Colitis Foundation of America's website,* **www.ccfa.org,** *and the Irritable Bowel Syndrome Association's website,* **www.ibsassociation.org.**

- *Remember, even famous people have IBD and IBS.* **John Kennedy had IBD** *since high school and went on to serve in the Navy, as a U.S. Senator and as the President of the United States.*

- **DO NOT** *let your illness stop you from achieving your goals or dreams.*

Epilogue

✦

2006

As I write this epilogue it has been four years since I wrote the last chapter of this book and I have continued to successfully live *with* IBD and IBS.

Yoga, meditation, and exercise have been added to my "tools" list and are an integral part of my continued success of living a healthy and happy life *with* IBD and IBS. Previously—between 1998 and 2002—my energy level was often so low that I simply stopped exercising. Time and time again my gastroenterologist urged me to exercise, explaining that the activity could actually help to improve my symptoms and my overall health. While I understood, and even agreed with, what he was saying I simply felt too tired and lethargic to act on his advice.

In 2003 when my husband was told by his doctor that he needed to lose 30 pounds to improve his cholesterol and blood pressure levels, he bought a family membership at a local gym. Simply knowing that the fee had already been paid made me feel that I had to use it in order not to waste the money. So, when my husband went to the gym, so did I. At first, I started out slowly—walking on the treadmill for 20 minutes at a time. A couple of weeks later I added 20 minutes of bicycling to my routine. Another two weeks went by and I met with one of the gym's trainers who helped me put together a weight lifting regimen to tone my long neglected muscles. Before I knew it, I was going to the gym three to four times per week and feeling great.

In fact, exercise has once again become a positive and needed part of my days. I also intersperse my gym workouts with walking, bicycling, and many other physical activities I can do with friends and family.

Yoga has also become an important part of my weekly routine. Not the power yoga that has become popular in the last couple of years, but traditional hatha yoga which focuses on stretching and toning the muscles. Three years ago I turned to the book, *Richard Hittleman's 28 day yoga exercise plan* to help get me into a yoga routine. I now alternate yoga days and exercise days and truly believe both have helped me to improve my emotional as well as my physical state of well-being.

◆   ◆   ◆

I have also come to realize that an adequate amount of sleep is imperative to my having a calm and happy gut. "Adequate" for me means a minimum of eight hours of sleep each night. When I can fit it in, nine hours of sleep is even better. On those occasions when I don't get an adequate amount of sleep I am almost assured of a gut that is rumbly and prone to lose stools and/or outright diarrhea.

My diet continues to be much the same—whole foods without preservatives or added ingredients. My gut has been relatively regular since June 2005 which has led me to try adding some things to my diet that I had previously eliminated because they caused cramps, bloating, or diarrhea.

Ever so slowly I introduced lettuce into my diet—the spring lettuce mix now available in stores—with just a touch of olive oil and salt. At first, things were hit and miss. On one occasion I could eat a small salad without problem. A week later I might try the same sized portion and loose stools or diarrhea would be back by the next morning. Currently, I am able to eat a small salad two or three times a week without major repercussions. However, I still will not eat any type of lettuce within a week of traveling, just in case it doesn't settle well.

Straying from the list of foods I know I can eat successfully is not without its troubles, though. At one point in 2005 I read a tip in a magazine suggesting that eating Concord grapes or drinking grape juice was a good way to increase your energy level. Increased energy is always something I can use so, on my next trip to the natural foods store I perused the bottled juices until I found a Concord grape juice that was just juice, no added sugars no preservatives (this is not an easy feat). Three days into drinking my one 8-oz. glass of grape juice per day I couldn't get out of the bathroom. Every thirty minutes I was back in the bathroom for most of the morning. I was so depleted of energy that I spent the afternoon on the couch trying to figure out what had triggered the flare up. I assessed my stress level, considered my diet, and finally concluded that the only possible culprit was the grape juice. I immediately stopped drinking the juice and within 24 hours my gut was back to normal. This was a perfect reminder to me to listen to my body. It was also a good lesson not to stray too far from the tried and proven foods and beverages that I know work with my body.

I am now also able to take vitamins on a regular basis—an adult multivitamin (my hair and fingernails have been growing like crazy since adding these to my daily routine), zinc (supposed to help increase energy and enhance immune response), and folic acid are now a part of my daily routine. I continue to take Asacol daily but, my current dose is less than half of the original dose I was taking in 1998—I am now taking the typical "maintenance" dose of the medication.

◆   ◆   ◆

Other things I can't stress enough when learning to live *with* IBD and IBS are to have and keep your sense of humor. Being able to make light of your situation can, and will, make you, and those around you, feel more comfortable with your situation—no matter what stage you're at with the disease.

IBD and IBS are much better known in the public arena today than they were five or ten years ago—I've actually seen TV ads for IBS medications, a Living with UC website, magazine ads for Crohn's disease, and, the CCFA even has wrist bands (a la Lance Armstrong) that you can purchase to help raise awareness of, and money for, IBD research.

Alternative medicine and therapies are also more available and accepted today than in past years. In fact, many health insurance companies now either include alternative therapies in their plans or have information about alternative practitioners who will offer discounts to certain health insurance company participants. For example, through my current health insurance company I receive discounts from "approved" alternative medicine practitioners. Acupuncture, hypnotherapy, and therapeutic massage are disciplines that can offer relief to some IBD and IBS sufferers. Stress-reduction workshops, yoga classes, or a few sessions with a dietician or nutritionist also can prove helpful in learning to live *with* IBD and IBS, and may be covered by your insurance.

◆   ◆   ◆

Take charge. Take charge of your condition and take charge of your life. Work with your doctors but also realize that they are humans, not miracle workers and they will not have a magic wand they can wave to make your symptoms disappear.

Each individual with IBD or IBS has different symptoms, different triggers, different levels of tolerance to the symptoms, and different solutions for feeling better. Begin today on your own journey to taking charge of your life and learning to live *with* your IBD or IBS.

Also, be patient. Be patient with yourself and with your body. When in the midst of a flare up it's hard not to be frustrated and angry with your body. Try to realize, even at the hardest and most painful times, that there is a reason why your body is doing what it's doing. Maybe it needs a break from the day-to-day hustle, maybe you strayed from those foods you know you can eat. Or, you may simply have to learn to accept that there is no logical explanation for a particular flare up. No matter what the reason might be, be patient with your body. Allow yourself to feel your feelings—be frustrated, angry, desperate, fatigued, exasperated—it's okay and nobody is going to judge you. Sometimes just acknowledging how you feel can actually help you to feel better by releasing stress that becomes trapped in our unexpressed emotions.

In the past few years I have received emails from a number of other IBD and IBS patients. Many of these emails deal with the frustration people have with their doctors' inability to "cure them," or "make their symptoms go away." Or, people simply don't want to take the advice their doctor has given them and instead write to me, and other IBD or IBS patients, looking for a magic bullet that will make them feel better.

One woman who wrote me was having a particular problem with bothersome cramping in her lower abdomen. She had consulted both her gastroenterologist and her gynecologist, and had tried taking various over-the-counter and prescription medications, all to no avail—she still had cramps. One of her doctors had recommended she keep a food journal to see if she could link her symptoms to any particular food or foods. She claimed she wasn't disciplined enough to keep a journal, and on days without cramps she didn't feel it was necessary.

In my answer to her email I told her I didn't think the cramps were bad enough or bothersome enough to her yet. *When they are so bad that you can't stand it you'll do everything and anything to figure out how to make them either lessen or go away all together*, I told her. I explained to her about my "poop journals" and how the elimination diet I had done so many years ago highlighted my "trigger" foods. I told her that when the cramps got bad enough she would make time in her life to keep not only a food journal but a life journal—a daily journal detailing what she ate, how she felt after eating it, her daily activities, stress levels, alcohol intake, physical symptoms, etc.

We all have different levels of pain, different levels of tolerance, and differences in how involved we want to be in achieving our own state of health and happiness. You can sit back, wait for a cure and let life go by without you. Or, you can take advantage of each good hour, day, week, or month you have and take control of you and the disease that is now a *part* of your life.

Even in the face of adversity be as positive as you can muster—things always look better with a positive attitude. Share your successes with your family, your friends, and especially with other IBD and IBS patients—we can all learn *something* from each other, if just that there are other people who understand our frustrations, feelings, successes, and failures. Knowing we are not alone is possibly the most important step in healing.

978-0-595-40293-9
0-595-40293-3

Printed in the United States
77810LV00002B/107